52 Country Projects for the Weekend Woodworker

John A. Nelson

Sterling Publishing Co., Inc.   New York

Dedication

To my grandson, Daniel John O'Rourke, a future woodworker

Acknowledgments

I am especially grateful to all those unknown early American craftsmen whose wonderful one-of-a-kind projects are featured throughout. Their designs are appreciated just as much today as in years past.

I want to thank Deborah Porter for taking all the photographs—I think she captured each of the projects just right.

I extend thanks to John Woodside, Editorial Director, Rodman Neumann, Editor, and the staff at STERLING PUBLISHING CO., who have transformed my manuscript and art into this finished book.

I also appreciate all the effort and help I've received from David Camp, Editor of *Popular Woodworking* magazine, who, unknowingly, helped me refine my work over the years.

I offer special appreciation and thanks to my wife, Joyce, for making some sense of my scribblings, my notes, and my poor English and for typing it into something sensible. She also did the painting for the painted projects.

Surely without the help of these people this book would never have been written or produced.

J.A.N.

Library of Congress Cataloging-in-Publication Data

Nelson, John A., 1935–
    52 country projects for the weekend woodworker / John A. Nelson.
       p. cm.
    Includes index.
    ISBN 0-8069-8625-5
    1. Woodwork. I. Title. II. Title: Fifty-two country projects
for the weekend woodworker.
    TT180.N42 1992
    684'.08—dc20   92-8580
                                           CIP

Edited by R. P. Neumann

10 9 8 7 6 5 4 3 2 1

Published in 1992 by Sterling Publishing Company, Inc.
387 Park Avenue South, New York, N.Y. 10016
© 1992 by John A. Nelson
Distributed in Canada by Sterling Publishing
% Canadian Manda Group, P.O. Box 920, Station U
Toronto, Ontario, Canada M8Z 5P9
Distributed in Great Britain and Europe by Cassell PLC
Villiers House, 41/47 Strand, London WC2N 5JE, England
Distributed in Australia by Capricorn Link Ltd.
P.O. Box 665, Lane Cove, NSW 2066
Manufactured in the United States of America
All rights reserved

Sterling ISBN 0-8069-8625-5

Contents

INTRODUCTION

Many books are written to make a statement: this book, however, is meant as a work of guidance and—more importantly—of preservation. As a guide for woodworkers, this volume is intended to help them reproduce authentic copies of "country" pieces. As a work of preservation, this volume achieves its higher purpose: to provide an accurate record of unusual, small objects, each of which is an antique that was once part of the everyday lives of those who used them so long ago.

The instructions and the drawings for each project allow the exact reproduction of the original antique. Each piece was found in the northeastern United States, ranging from Pennsylvania to New England. No attempt has been made to improve or update the original construction methods used, even if they could be improved using tools or methods that are available today. The original makers created one-of-a-kind pieces, often using only very limited hand tools and not necessarily very great skills.

For each project, when known, the original wood that was used is indicated. If the piece was painted, its color and specifics are also given in as much detail as possible. Adding a wash coat (as explained under "Achieving a 150-Year-Old Look") will give your reproduction a finish that will look like the antique on which it's based.

One or two projects have been scaled down slightly for the smaller homes of today. If the finished dimensions of a project have been reduced, it has been noted.

In days past, each of these pieces served a particular, important need. Needs have changed, but, nevertheless, each of these pieces in reproduction can find a place in our lives that is equally functional.

The projects have been carefully chosen so that only basic woodworking tools are necessary. The craftsperson with very limited space or only basic woodworking tools can make any of these pieces. With the possible exception of a few wooden knobs or drawer pulls, a lathe is not necessary. Even then, manufactured wooden knobs, very close to the original style, are widely available today.

Because each reader will be at a different skill level and each will have different tools, only very brief and basic instructions for making each project are given in most cases. Most projects are rather simple and, with a little thought and preparation, should be within the skill level of most woodworkers. Each piece should be able to be put together over a weekend, with an extra day or two to apply a stain or paint finish.

However, before starting work on any project, carefully study the drawings provided so that you fully understand *exactly* how it is to be made and assembled. The exploded-view drawing, provided with each project where appropriate, illustrates exactly how it is to be assembled—be sure you fully understand how it is assembled before starting.

I have made every effort to clearly and fully illustrate each project—and each individual part as necessary. Each dimension has been checked and rechecked to make your work go smoothly and quickly.

Using the Drawings for Each Project

With each project there is at least a two-view drawing provided. One is almost always called the *front view,* and the other is either the *side view* or the *top view.* These views are positioned in a standard way; the front view is always the most important view and the place you should start in studying the drawings. The side view is located directly to the *right* of the front view; the top view is located directly *above* the front view.

At times a *section view* is used to further illustrate some particular feature(s) of the project. The section view is sometimes a partial view that illustrates only a portion of the project such as a particular moulding detail or way of joining parts.

Most of the projects also have an *exploded view,* which fully illustrates how the project goes together. Make sure that *you* fully understand how the project is to be assembled *before* any work is started.

The drawings throughout this book *number* each and every part. Each part is called-off in as many views as possible so that you can see *exactly* where each part is located. A box accompanies each set of drawings that serves as a *bill of materials* list. Each part is listed, *in order,* using the same number *and* noting its name, its overall size, and exactly *how many* of each part is required.

Multiple parts should be made exactly the same size and shape. Every now and then a project requires a *pair* of parts, that is, a right-hand piece and a left-hand piece. In such a case, take care not to make duplicate pieces, but rather a left-hand and right-hand pair. In most projects requiring a pair, this is noted—but for any "multiple" parts double-check if in doubt.

Throughout, when practical, I numbered all the parts in the order that I would *suggest* you make and assemble them. You might want to make and assemble your project some other way, but this is what worked best for me and is how I made it.

Making the Project

After you thoroughly study the project, start by carefully making each individual part. Take care to make each piece exactly to the correct size and exactly *square*—that is, each cut at 90 degrees to the face—as required.

Sand each individual piece, but take care to keep all the edges sharp— **do not round the edges** at this time—some will be rounded *after* assembly.

After all the pieces have been made with great care, "dry-fit" the pieces— that is, cautiously put together the entire project to check for correct fit throughout before final assembly. If anything needs refitting, this is the time to correct it.

When the pieces all fit correctly, glue and/or nail the project together, again taking care that all fits are tight and square. Sand the project all over; it is at this time that edges can be "rounded," if necessary. The project is then ready for finishing.

Today, the trend is towards using the metric system of measure; therefore, a Metric Conversion chart is provided for quick conversion on page 160.

Enlarging a Pattern or Design

Many of the drawings are reduced relative to the actual size of the parts so that all of the information can be presented on the page. In some projects, the patterns for irregular parts or irregular portions of parts must be enlarged to full size. A grid of squares is drawn over these parts and the original size of the grid is noted on the drawing.

There are four ways a design or shape of the irregular part or parts can be enlarged to full size.

Method One

One of the simplest and most inexpensive ways is to use an ordinary office-type photocopy machine. Most of these newer machines have an enlarging/reducing feature. Simply put the book page on the machine, choose the enlargement mode you need (usually expressed as a percentage of the original), and make a copy. In extreme cases, you may have to make *another* copy of the enlargement copy in order to get the required size—sometimes you must make more than two copies. In some cases you will not be able to get the exact required size but the result will be close enough for most work, perhaps requiring a little touching up, at most.

Method Two

A very quick and extremely accurate method is to go to a local commercial "Quick-Printer" and ask them to make a P.M.T. (photomechanical transfer) of the area needed to be enlarged or reduced. This is a photographic method that yields an *exact* size without any difficulty. This method will cost about five to fifteen dollars, depending on the size of the final P.M.T.—if your time is valuable, it might be worth the cost.

Method Three

Another simple, quick method is to use a drawing tool called the *pantograph*. It is an inexpensive tool that is very simple to use for enlarging or reducing to almost any required size. If you do a lot of enlarging or reducing, the cost of this tool may be well worth the price.

Method Four

Most authors assume woodworkers will use the grid and dot-to-dot method. It is very simple; you do not have to be an artist to use the method. This method can be used to enlarge or reduce to *any size* or scale. This method requires eight simple steps:

Step 1: Note what size the full-size grid should be—this is usually indicated on the drawing near the grid. Most of the grids used with the project drawings must be redrawn so that each square is one-half inch or one inch per side.

Step 2: Calculate the overall required width and height. If it is *not* given, simply count the squares across and down and multiply by the size of each square. For example, a one-half-inch grid with 15 squares across requires an overall width of 7½ inches. The paper size needed to draw the pattern full size should be a little larger than the overall size of the part.

Step 3: Note: It would be helpful if you have a few basic drafting tools, but not necessary. Tools suggested are: a drafting board, a scale (ruler), a T-square, a 45-degree triangle, masking tape, and a sheet of paper a little larger than the required overall size of the pattern. Tape the paper to the drafting board or other surface and carefully draw the required grid on the paper using the drafting tools or whatever tools you have.

Step 4: On the original reduced drawing in the book, start from the upper left corner and add *letters* across the top of the grid from left to right, A through whatever letter it takes to get to the other side of the grid. From the same starting point, add *numbers* down, from 1 to whatever number it takes to get to the bottom of the grid.

Step 5: On your full-size grid, add letters and numbers in exactly the same way as the original.

Step 6: On the original reduced drawing, draw dots along the pattern outline wherever it crosses the grid.

Step 7: On your full-size grid, locate and draw the same dots on the grid. It is helpful to locate each dot by using the letters across the top and the numbers along the side. For example, a dot at B-6 can easily be found on the new, full-size grid by coming down from line B and over on line 6.

Step 8: All that is left to do is to connect the dots. Note: you do not have to be exact, all you have to do is to sketch a line between the dots using your eye to approximate the shape of the original reduced drawing.

Transferring the Pattern from Paper to Wood

Tape the full-size pattern to the wood with carbon paper in between for transferring the pattern. If you are going to copy the pattern many times, make a template instead. Simply transfer the pattern onto a sheet of heavy cardboard or ⅛-inch-thick hardboard or plywood and cut out the pattern. This template can then be used over and over by simply tracing around the template to lay out the pattern for each copy.

If the pattern is symmetrical—that is, the exact same size and shape on both sides of an imaginary line—make only a *half-pattern* and trace it twice, once on each side of the midline. This will ensure the perfect symmetry of the finished part.

For small patterns—8½ inches by 11 inches or smaller at full size—make a photocopy of the full-size pattern using any copy machine. Tape the copy, printed side down, and using a hot flatiron or hot wood-burning set, heat the back side of the copy. The pattern will transfer from the paper directly to the wood. This method is very good for very small or complicated patterns.

Again, for small patterns—8½ inches by 11 inches or smaller at full size—make a photocopy of the pattern. Using rubber cement or spray-mount adhesive, lightly glue the copy directly to the wood. Cut out the piece with the copy glued directly to the wood. Simply peel the copy from the wood *after* you cut out the piece. Then sand all over.

Selecting Material for Your Project

As lumber will probably be the most expensive material you will purchase for each project, it is a good idea that you have some basic knowledge about lumber so that you can make wise choices and save a little money here and there on your purchases.

All lumber is divided into two kinds, hardwood and softwood. Hardwoods are deciduous trees, trees that flower and lose their leaves seasonally; softwoods are the coniferous trees, which are cone-bearing and mostly evergreen. In actuality, a few "hardwoods" are softer than some "softwoods"—but on the whole, hardwoods are harder, closer grained, much more durable, tougher to work, and take a stain beautifully. Hardwood typically costs more than softwood, but it is well worth it.

All wood contains pores—open spaces that served as water-conducting vessels—which are more noticeable in some kinds than in others. Woods such as oak and mahogany have pores that are very noticeable and probably should be filled, for the best finished appearance. Woods such as maple and birch have what is called close-grain, which provides a beautiful smooth finish.

The *grain* of wood is the result of each year's growth of new cells. Around the tree's circumference each year annular growth forms a new and hard fibrous layer. Growth in most trees is seasonal but somewhat regular, so that these rings are evenly spaced. In other trees this annular growth is not very regular, thus creating uneven spacing and thickness. The patterns formed by the rings when the tree is cut into lumber is what we see as the grain pattern.

The softwoods I used for most of the projects are pine, spruce, and fir. Pine was the favorite since it is the easiest to work, especially for simple accessories such as those found in this book. The hardwoods I used most were maple, walnut, oak, cherry, poplar, and birch.

Always buy "dried" lumber, as "green" lumber will shrink, twist, and warp while drying. Purchase the best lumber you can find for these projects since each of them does not take much material at all. Your work will be much easier and the finished project will be so much better for the better quality wood. The actual cost difference between an inexpensive piece of wood and the best you can find will be quite small since the overall cost of any of these projects is very low to begin with.

A few projects call for wide boards. I believe the project would look best if you could find the correct width. The correct width also adds to the authenticity. If this is not possible, glue narrower boards together by edge-joining them to produce the necessary width. Try to match grain patterns with great care so that each joint will not be so noticeable. Even though I prefer the look of the single wide board, I should point out that a glued joint is as strong as a single piece of wood and probably will not warp.

Kinds of Joint

The projects require four kinds of joint—and, for the most part, only three. These basic joints are the *butt joint*, the *rabbet joint*, the *dado joint* and, in a few instances, the *dovetail joint*. These can be made by hand, without power tools. If you do have the power tools, use them; early crafters would have used them if *they* had them.

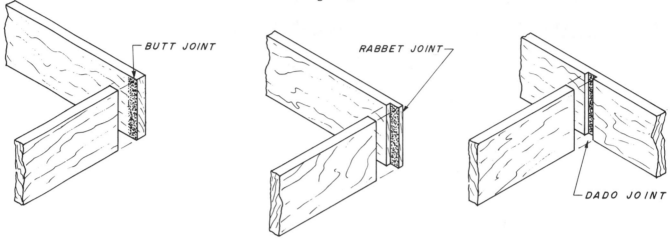

Most of the simpler projects use the *butt joint*. This is the simplest of all joints and, as its name implies, is simply two boards that are butted up against each other and joined together, perhaps with glue and nails or screws. The major disadvantage of the butt joint is that there is less surface area available for gluing or nailing than for other joints. Nails sometimes back out of the joint over time, which also makes an opening at the joint. A *rabbet joint* is an L-shaped cutout made along the edge or end of one board to overlap the edge or end of the mating board. This joint can also be nailed and/or glued together. Because rabbet joints are often cut into side pieces, the nails—put in from the sides—may be hidden somewhat from view. *Dado joints* are similar to rabbet joints, except that the cut is made leaving wood shoulders on both sides. A drawer side is an excellent example of the use of both a dado joint and a rabbet joint.

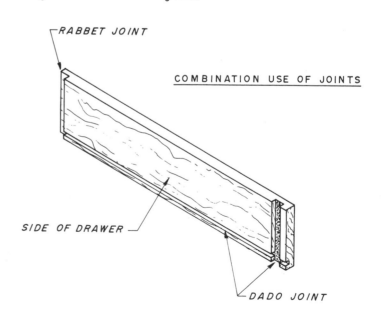

Gluing

Glue was not in general use until after 1750. Therefore, most of the projects featured in this book probably were simply nailed together. If by chance they were glued together, they were probably glued together with "hot" animal—or hide—glue.

Wood glues are either "hot" or "cold" glue, depending whether or not heat is used to prepare them. The "hot" glue is made from animal parts, which make the glue very strong and quick-setting. Until very recently old-fashioned hide glue was considered the *only* true, satisfactory kind of glue to use in cabinetmaking. Recent developments in new and better "cold" glues have made this generalization debatable. Cold glues are all derived from synthetic material of one kind or another. They vary in durability and strength. For the simpler projects cold glue is, by far, the easiest to use, and I recommend its use. In using cold glue, always follow the instructions given on the label.

When gluing, always take care to clean all excess glue from around the joint. This is a *must* if you are going to stain the project. The excess glue will not take the stain and will appear white. I find that by waiting for 10 to 15 minutes, just until the glue is almost set, I can carefully remove most of it with a sharp wood chisel. Do not wipe off the excessive glue with a wet cloth as the water will weaken the glue joint and possibly spread glue into the pore space irretrievably, staining the wood.

For the few projects that are a little difficult to hold together properly while gluing, the new hot-glue guns can be very helpful. Hot-glue guns use solid glue sticks that are inserted, heated to their melting point, and then liquid glue is pushed through the tip while very hot. This kind of glue dries very quickly and sets in about 10 seconds without clamping. Take care if you use this kind of glue as it is difficult to get good tight-fitting joints every time. The glue sets up so quickly that you have to work very quickly. This kind of glue is good to use for special applications but not for everything; the slower-drying cold glue is still better to use for most of the projects.

Finishing

Once you have completed assembling your project, you are then ready to apply a finish. This is the important part and should not be rushed. Remember, this is the part that will make the biggest impression for many years to come. No matter how good the wood and hardware you use, regardless of how good the joints are, a poor finish will ruin your project. If it takes eight hours to make the project, plan on eight hours to finish it correctly.

Preparing

Step 1: All joints should be checked for tight fits. If necessary apply water putty to all joints—allow ample time for drying. As these are "country" projects, it is not necessary to set and fill the nail heads as most of the originals were left with the nail heads showing. If, however, you do not want to see the nail heads, then set and apply water putty to fill those nail heads, also.

Step 2: Sand the project all over in the direction of the wood grain. If sanding is done by hand, use a sanding block, and be careful to keep all corners still *sharp*. Sand all over using an 80 grit sandpaper. Resand all over using a 120 grit sandpaper, and, if necessary, sand once more with 180 grit sandpaper. Take care not to "round" edges at this time.

Step 3: If you do want any of the edges rounded, use the 120 grit sandpaper, and later the 180 grit sandpaper, specifically to round the edges.

Step 4: I personally think the "country" projects should look old. A copy of an antique that looks new seems somehow to be a direct contradiction. Distressing—making the piece look old—can be done in many ways. Using a piece of coral stone about three inches in diameter, or a similar object, roll the stone across the various surfaces. Don't be afraid to add a few random scratches here and there, especially on the bottom or back, where an object would have been worn the most. Carefully study the object, and try to imagine how it would have been used through the years. Using a rasp, judiciously round the edges where you think wear would have occurred. Resand the entire project and the new "worn" edges with 180 grit paper.

Step 5: Clean all surfaces with a damp rag to remove all dust.

Staining

There are two major kinds of stain: water-base stain and oil-base stain. Water stains are commonly purchased in powder form and mixed as needed by dissolving the powder in hot water. Premixed water-base stains have recently become available. Water stain has a tendency to raise the grain of the wood, so that after it dries, the surface should be lightly sanded with fine sandpaper. Oil stain is made from pigments ground in linseed oil and does not raise the grain.

Fillers

A paste filler should be used for porous wood such as oak, ash, or mahogany. Purchase paste filler that is slightly darker than the color of your wood as the new wood you used will turn darker with age. Before using paste filler, thin it with turpentine so it can be applied with a brush. Use a stiff brush, and brush with the grain in order to fill the pores. Wipe off with a piece of burlap across the grain after 15 or 20 minutes, taking care to leave filler in the pores. Apply a second coat if necessary; let it dry for 24 hours.

Step 1: Test the stain color on a scrap piece of the same kind of lumber to make certain it will be the color you wish.

Step 2: Wipe or brush on the stain as quickly and as even as possible to avoid overlapping streaks. If a darker finish is desired, apply more than one coat of stain. Try not to apply too much stain on the end grain. Allow to dry in a dust-free area for at least 24 hours.

Finishes

Shellac is a hard, easy-to-apply finish and dries in a few hours. For best results, thin slightly with alcohol and apply an extra coat or two. Several coats of thin shellac are much better than one or two thick coats. Sand lightly with extra-fine sandpaper between coats, but be sure to rub the entire surface with a dampened cloth. Strive for a smooth, satin finish—not a high-gloss finish coat—for that "antique" effect.

Varnish is easy to brush on and dries to a smooth, hard finish within 24 hours. It makes an excellent finish that is transparent and will give a deep finish look to your project. Be sure to apply varnish in a completely dust-free area. Apply one or two coats directly from the can with long, even strokes. Rub between each coat, and after the last coat, with 0000 steel wool.

Oil finishes are especially easy to use for projects such as those in this book. Oil finish is easy to apply, long-lasting, never needs resanding, actually improves wood permanently. Apply a heavy, wet coat uniformly to all surfaces, and let set for 20 or 30 minutes. Wipe completely dry until you have a pleasing finish.

Painted Projects

Use a high-quality paint, either oil or water base. Today, the trend is towards water-base paint. Prime your project, and lightly sand after it dries. Apply two *light* coats of paint rather than one thick coat. I like to add some water to thin water-base paint since I feel that water-base paint tends to be a little thick. For all projects for children, be sure to use a nontoxic paint at all times.

Note: For a very satisfying "feel" to the finish and professional touch to your project, apply a top-coat of paste wax as the final step.

Achieving a 150-Year-Old Look

Follow the five steps outlined for preparing your project as described above under finishing. Then follow these steps to distress your project.

Step 1: Seal the wood with a light coat of shellac with 50% alcohol. After the shellac is dry, rub lightly with 0000 steel wool. Wipe clean.

Step 2: Apply an even coat of oil-base paint, taking care to use an antique color paint. Let dry for 48 hours. Do not paint the backs or bottoms—these were seldom painted on the original pieces.

Step 3: Sand with 120 grit sandpaper all the rounded edges you prepared for "wear" marks in "Preparing" step 4. Remember, if these edges were worn, the paint surely would have been removed, also. Sand away paint from all sharp edges and corners since edges and corners would wear through the years.

Step 4: Lightly sand all over to remove any paint gloss, using 180 grit sandpaper. Wipe clean.

Step 5: Wipe on a *wash coat* of oil-base, black paint with a cloth directly from the can. Take care to get the black paint in all corners, and in all distress marks and scratches. Don't forget the unpainted back and bottoms. Wipe all paint off immediately before it dries, but leave black paint in all corners, joints, scratches, and distress marks. If you apply too much, wipe off using a cloth with turpentine on it. Let dry for 24 hours. Apply a light coat of paste wax.

Alternative One

For that "extra" aged look, apply two coats of paint—each a totally different color; for example, first coat, a powder blue; second coat, antique brick red. Allow 24 hours between coats. After the second coat has dried for 48 hours or more, follow steps 3 and 4 above, but sand the top coat off so that the first color shows through here and there, in layers at worn areas. Finish up with step 5 as outlined above. This is especially good on projects such as footstools or large painted wall boxes.

Alternative Two

If you want your painted project to have a "crackled" finish, follow these additional steps. After step 1 above, apply a coat of liquid hide glue over the intended painted surfaces. Let dry four to twelve hours. Then paint on a coat of gesso (a form of base paint in use since the sixteenth century). Paint lightly and do not go over any strokes. In 10 to 15 seconds, the gesso will start to crackle. Let dry for 24 hours in a very dry area. After 24 hours or more, continue on to step 2 above. (It would be a good idea to experiment on scrap wood before applying any of this to your finished project. Some craftworkers combine step 2 with the crackling by mixing their paint with the gesso, two parts gesso to one part paint.)

Visits to museums, antique shops, and flea markets will help you develop an eye for exactly what an original antique looks like. This will give you an excellent idea of how antiques were worn through the years. With this firsthand experience, you will have a much clearer idea of what kind of finish you are after, so that your careful reproduction will realistically look 150 years old.

THE 52 COUNTRY PROJECTS

COUNTRY HOUSEHOLD PROJECTS

1 ◆ Pie Peel

This pattern based on a pie peel blends in well with any early American setting. Today you probably do not have much use for a pie peel as such, but the pattern does make a *great* cutting board. Simply tie a leather strap in the ½-inch diameter hole, and hang your reproduction on the wall—ready for use, although not in the oven.

Instructions

Since the pattern is somewhat irregular in shape, the outline should be laid out carefully, using the given dimensions to make a full-size pattern. Lay out the shape, full size, on a piece of heavy paper, cardboard, or directly on the wood itself.

Carefully cut out the shape, and lightly sand the top and bottom surfaces and around the edge with medium sandpaper to remove any burrs and all tool marks. Take care to keep *all* edges square and sharp.

If you are making the project actually as a pie peel, taper the front surface to three-eighths-inch thick, as shown in the side view. If you prefer to use the piece as a cutting board, simply leave the board at its full thickness throughout its length.

When transferring the full-size pattern to the board, check all dimensions for accuracy before cutting the shape out. Resand all over with fine grit sandpaper, being careful still to keep all edges sharp.

Finishing

If you are making a reproduction of the pie peel for display only, you can select most any satin finish that appeals to you. If you are making this as a cutting board for actual use, be sure to use a nontoxic finish, such as one labelled "salad bowl" finish. I sometimes use salad oil from the kitchen, although some woodworkers say it can become rancid, and, therefore, should *not* be used. I've always had good luck with it.

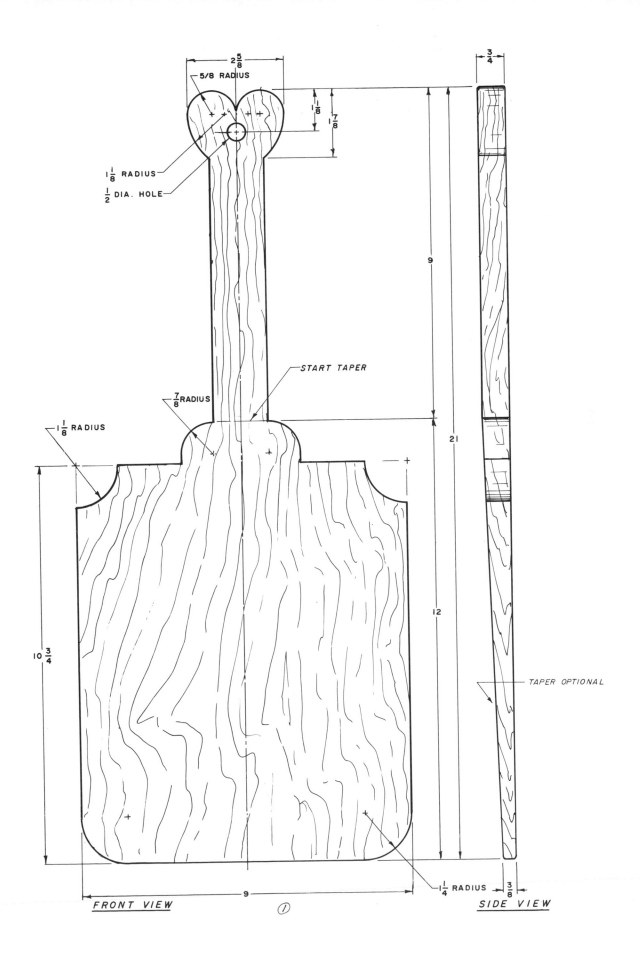

2 5/8

5/8 RADIUS

1 1/8 RADIUS

1/2 DIA. HOLE

1 1/8

1 7/8

9

START TAPER

7/8 RADIUS

1 1/8 RADIUS

21

3/4

TAPER OPTIONAL

12

10 3/4

1 1/4 RADIUS

3/8

9

1 1/4 RADIUS

FRONT VIEW   ①   _SIDE VIEW_

2♦Hand Mirror

Here is a formal hand mirror for which you can get some practice on your lathe as you try to reproduce it. The original piece in which the mirror is set is made of four separate pieces. I did the same for my copy, but if I were to make another, I would use only *one* piece of wood. This would *not* be an accurate reproduction of the original, but it would be much easier to make. Construction would be much faster, and it would look as good— probably it actually would be stronger, too. This project does not take much material, so use the best wood you can get. I used bird's-eye maple for mine.

Instructions

Study the plans carefully. Note how the mirror is put together. Try to visualize how you will turn the parts on your lathe.

Carefully cut all of the parts to size according to the materials list. Try to use wood with a pleasing grain pattern.

If you decide in favor of ''authenticity'' using the four segments as shown, cut the four segments, and then glue them together. Be sure you have good tight joints all around. Each segment is ¾ inch thick by 2 inches wide, and 7⅜ inches long. After turning on the lathe, the assembly should be ⅝ inch thick, as noted.

Sand the top and bottom surfaces with medium sandpaper to get a nicely smooth, flat back. Mount the four, glued-up segments to the lathe, and turn the assembly according to the given dimensions.

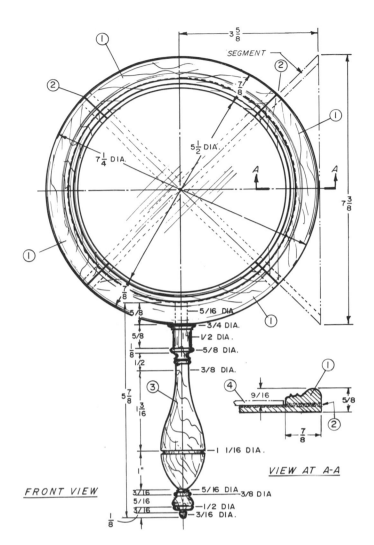

NO.	NAME	SIZE	REQ'D.
1*	SEGMENT	5/8 x 3 5/8 - 7 3/8 LG.	4
2	SPLINE	1/8 X 1/2 - 2 1/4 LG.	4
3	HANDLE	1 1/8 DIA. X 8 LONG	1
4	MIRROR	6 DIA.	1

*OPTIONAL FOUR PIECES -- 5/8 X 7 3/8 - 7 3/8 LG.
ONE PIECE

FRONT VIEW

VIEW AT A-A

Important: *Be sure to wait at least 24 hours* before turning. *Be sure to wear a face mask* when turning a segmented part such as this one. I had a project like this one come apart while turning, because I did not let the glue set long enough.

Finish the mirror-back assembly while still on the lathe. Locate and carefully drill a 5/16-inch-diameter hole about 5/8 inch deep, as shown.

Turn the handle according to the given dimensions. Be sure to leave a 5/16-inch-diameter "tenon" at the top end for mounting to the mirror. Finish the handle while it's still on the lathe.

Glue the mirror in place *after* the parts have been finished and then assembled.

3♦Scoop with Handle

I wonder just *how* old this project really is, but it *was* in an antique shop and it did *look* old. For those who like rosemaling and tole painting, this scoop makes a great project.

If you do not have a lathe, a suitable handle can be purchased.

Instructions

Study the plans carefully to see how each part is to be made. Try to *visualize* how you will make *each* part with the tools you have.

Carefully cut all of the parts to size according to the materials list. Take care to cut all parts to exact size, keeping them precisely square (90 degrees). *Stop and recheck all dimensions before going on.*

Lightly sand all surfaces and edges with medium sandpaper to remove any burrs and all tool marks. Take care to keep *all* edges square and sharp at this time. Recheck all dimensions for accuracy, and then resand all over with fine grit sandpaper, still keeping all edges sharp.

After the pieces have been carefully made, dry-fit the parts—that is, put the project together without glue or nails to check for accuracy and good-fitting joints. If anything needs refitting, now is the time to correct it.

Once all of the parts fit together correctly, assemble the project, being careful to keep everything square as you go. Once again check that all fits are tight.

Finishing

Finish to suit, following the general finishing instructions given in the introduction.

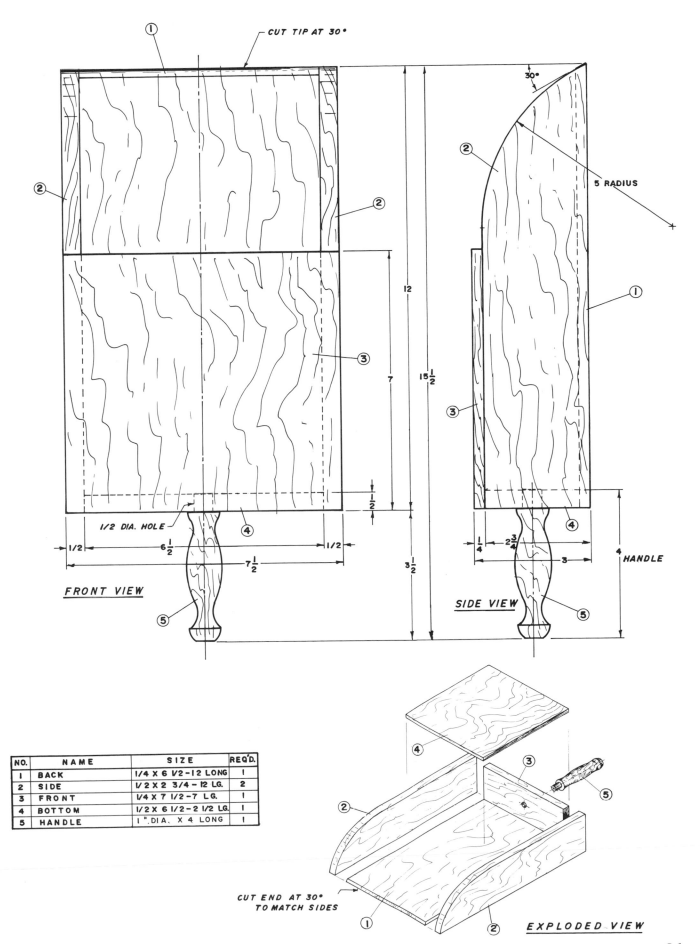

CUT TIP AT 30°

① ② ③ ④ ⑤ ②

30°

5 RADIUS

12

15 1/2

7

1/2

3 1/2

1/2 DIA. HOLE

1/2   6 1/2   1/2

7 1/2

FRONT VIEW

1/4   2 3/4

3

4

HANDLE

SIDE VIEW

NO.	NAME	SIZE	REQ'D.
I	BACK	1/4 X 6 1/2 - 12 LONG	1
2	SIDE	1/2 X 2 3/4 - 12 LG.	2
3	FRONT	1/4 X 7 1/2 - 7 LG.	1
4	BOTTOM	1/2 X 6 1/2 - 2 1/2 LG.	1
5	HANDLE	1" DIA. X 4 LONG	1

CUT END AT 30°
TO MATCH SIDES

EXPLODED VIEW

21

4♦Silver Tray

I cannot understand why the silver tray is not used much anymore. I made one for my wife years ago, and she has used it ever since. Each of my two married daughters had to have one for her new home. I have since made trays for most of our friends.

These old silver trays are still very handy—to hold silverware. Like the footstool, silver trays come in all shapes and sizes. They range from somewhat crude to very formal. Some were painted and others simply stained.

For a somewhat formal tray such as this one, I recommend a hardwood such as cherry, maple, or walnut.

Instructions

Study the plans carefully. Note how each part is to be shaped. As you study the plans, try to *visualize* how you will make each part and then how the project will be assembled. Note which parts you will put together first, second, and so on—exactly how *you* will put them together.

The center and end pieces, parts number 1 and 2, are irregular in shape and will have to be laid out on a ½-inch grid to make a full-size pattern. Lay out the full-size grid on heavy paper or cardboard, and transfer the shape of the piece to the grid, point by point.

Transfer the full-size patterns to the wood, and carefully cut out the pieces. Check all dimensions for accuracy. Sand all over with fine grit sandpaper, keeping all edges sharp.

Using a router and a ³⁄₁₆-inch-radius cutter with a ball-bearing follower, make a ³⁄₁₆-inch radius around the inside and outer edges of the center and end pieces, parts number 1 and 2. Be sure to start and stop the cut as shown in the detail plans.

Carefully cut the other parts to size according to the materials list. Take care to cut these parts to exact size.

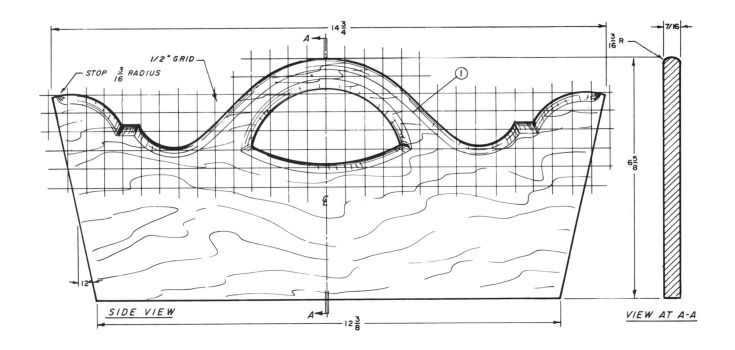

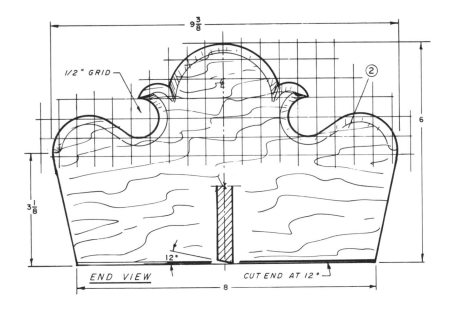

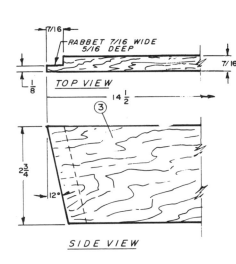

Note: The bottom edges of the ends and sides, parts number 2 and 3, are cut at 12 degrees, as shown. Carefully cut a ⁷⁄₁₆-inch-wide by ⁵⁄₁₆-inch-deep rabbet on the ends of the side pieces at 12 degrees.

Lightly sand all surfaces and edges with medium sandpaper to remove all tool marks. Take care to keep *all* edges square and sharp.

After all of the pieces have been carefully made, dry-fit the parts—that is, put the complete project together without glue or nails to check for accuracy and good-fitting joints. If anything needs refitting, now is the time to correct it.

Once all of the parts fit together correctly, assemble the center, end, and sides with square-cut finish nails. Check that all joints are tight. Sand the bottom edges flat before adding the bottom piece, part number 5. With addition of the bottom piece your silver tray is ready to finish.

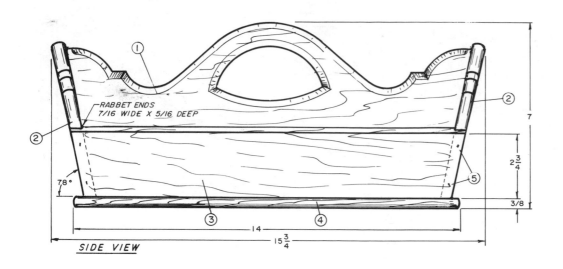

① RABBET ENDS
7/16 WIDE X 5/16 DEEP

② ②

78°

SIDE VIEW

7

2 3/4

3/8

③ ④ ⑤

14

15 3/4

NO.	NAME	SIZE	REQ'D.
1	CENTER	7/16 X 6 5/8 –14 3/4 LG.	1
2	END	7/16 X 6 — 9 3/8 LG.	2
3	SIDE	7/16 X 2 3/4 –14 1/2 LG.	2
4	BOTTOM	3/8 X 9 –14 LONG	1
5	NAIL – FINISH	1" LONG (SQ. CUT)	26

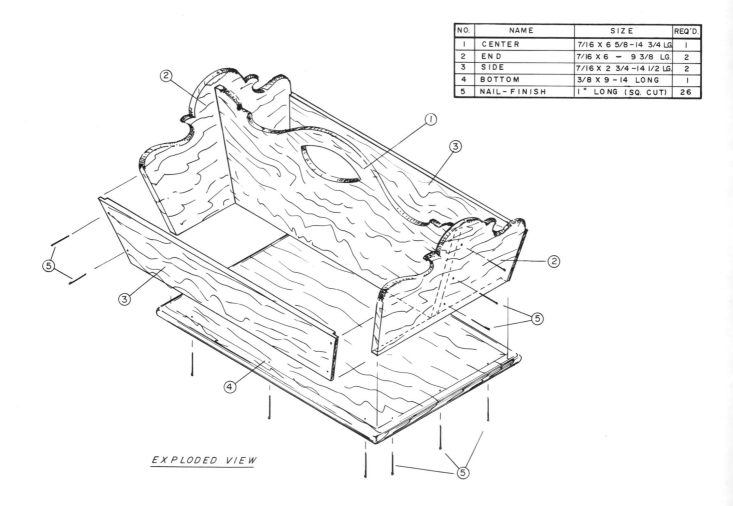

EXPLODED VIEW

Finishing

Finish to suit, following the general finishing instructions given in the introduction.

5 ♦ Tool Box

This is one of my favorite projects in this book. It is easy to make, has beautiful lines, can be made from scrap wood, and the finished project is extremely useful. But, perhaps I like it most of all because it becomes a hot item at craft shows.

These plans are based exactly on an original tool box, but I scaled it down to three-quarters—or 75 percent—of the original size. The original was painted, but you can either stain or paint yours.

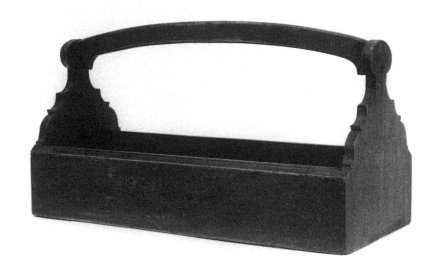

For garden Tools

Instructions

Study the plans carefully. Note how each part is to be shaped. As you study the plans, try to *visualize* how you will make each part, and then how the project will be assembled. Note which parts you will put together first, second, and so on—exactly how *you* will put them together.

The ends and handle, parts number 1 and 4, are irregular in shape and will have to be laid out on ½-inch grids to make full-size patterns. Lay out the full-size grids on heavy paper or cardboard, and transfer the shape of each piece to the grids, point by point.

Transfer the full-size patterns to the wood, and carefully cut out the pieces. Check all dimensions for accuracy. Sand all over with fine grit sandpaper, keeping all edges sharp.

Carefully cut the other parts to size according to the materials list. Take care to cut all of the parts to exact size, keeping them precisely square (90 degrees). *Stop and recheck all dimensions before going on.*

The sides, parts number 2, have a moulded top edge. If you have a router, rout a shape as close as you can to the one shown.

Lightly sand all surfaces and edges with medium sandpaper to remove all tool marks. Take care to keep *all* edges square and sharp.

After all of the pieces have been carefully made, dry-fit the parts. If anything needs refitting, now is the time to correct it.

Once all of the parts fit together correctly, assemble the project, keeping everything square as you go. Check that all fits are tight.

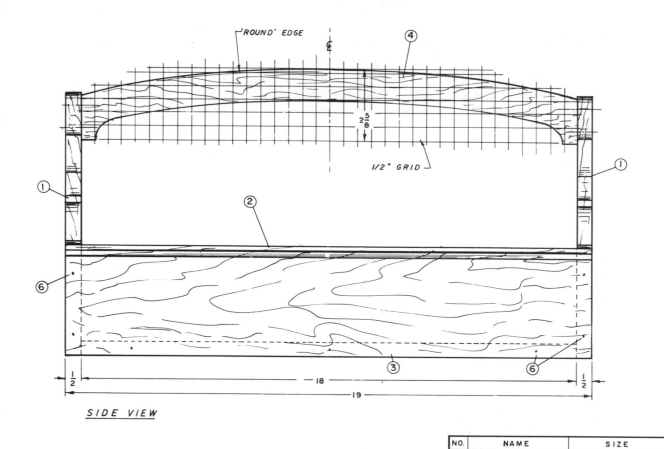

SIDE VIEW

NO.	NAME	SIZE	REQ'D.
1	END	1/2 X 7 1/8 – 9 1/2	2
2	SIDE	1/2 X 4 – 19 LONG	2
3	BOTTOM	1/2 X 7 1/8 – 18 LG.	1
4	HANDLE	5/8 X 2 5/8 – 18 LG.	1
5	SCREW – FL. HD.	NO. 6 X 1 1/4 LG.	4
6	NAIL – FINISH	6 d	18

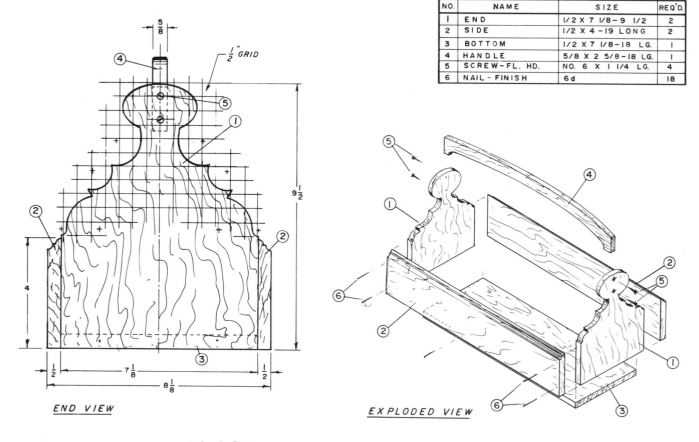

END VIEW

EXPLODED VIEW

Finishing

Finish to suit, following the general finishing instructions given in the introduction.

6◆Early American Lantern

I had always wanted an original antique wooden lantern, but could never afford one. The few I had seen for sale seemed prohibitively expensive and were not in all that great condition. I came upon this lantern at last, and I discovered that it is not very difficult to make and really adds a lot to any room it is hung in.

Instructions

Study the plans carefully. Note how each part is to be shaped. As you study the plans, try to *visualize* how you will make each part.

The handle, part number 9, should be steam-bent. I have seen this done and am pretty sure I could do it, but for this project I used an alternative approach. I simply cut 1/16-inch-thick strips about 9/16-inch wide. Then I glued them together over a 3/4-inch-thick by 3 3/4-inch-wide board. I cut this board into the shape of the *interior* of the bend. I then sanded the sides smooth to get the same 1/2-inch-wide handle as the original had. If you are set up to steam-bend the handle, then do—if not, simply glue up the 1/16-inch strips as I did. It is easy and really doesn't look like strips after the handle is sanded and finished.

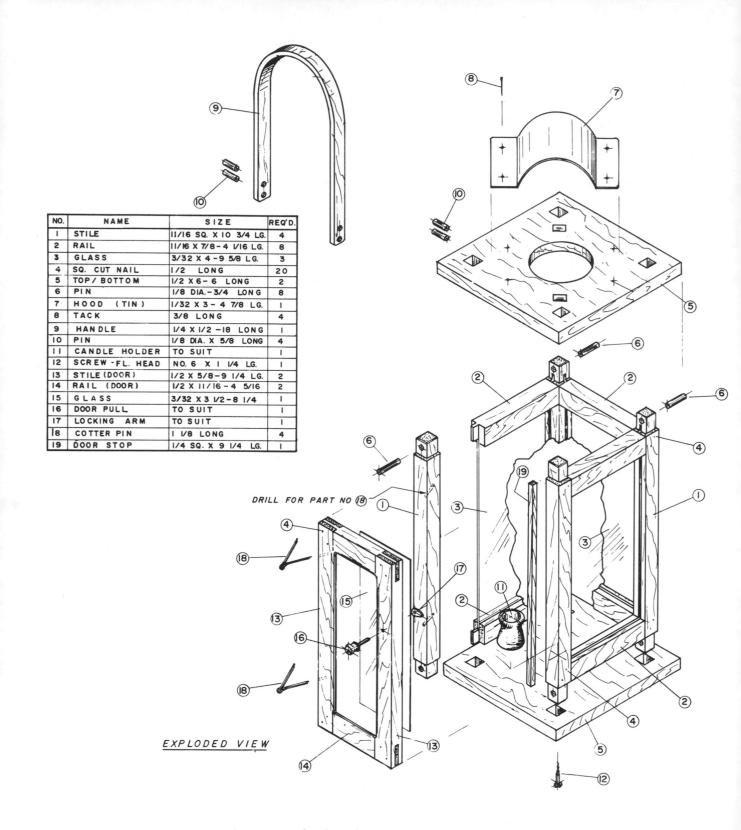

NO.	NAME	SIZE	REQ'D.
1	STILE	11/16 SQ. X 10 3/4 LG.	4
2	RAIL	11/16 X 7/8 - 4 1/16 LG.	8
3	GLASS	3/32 X 4 - 9 5/8 LG.	3
4	SQ. CUT NAIL	1/2 LONG	20
5	TOP / BOTTOM	1/2 X 6 - 6 LONG	2
6	PIN	1/8 DIA. - 3/4 LONG	8
7	HOOD (TIN)	1/32 X 3 - 4 7/8 LG.	1
8	TACK	3/8 LONG	4
9	HANDLE	1/4 X 1/2 - 18 LONG	1
10	PIN	1/8 DIA. X 5/8 LONG	4
11	CANDLE HOLDER	TO SUIT	1
12	SCREW - FL. HEAD	NO. 6 X 1 1/4 LG.	1
13	STILE (DOOR)	1/2 X 5/8 - 9 1/4 LG.	2
14	RAIL (DOOR)	1/2 X 11/16 - 4 5/16	2
15	GLASS	3/32 X 3 1/2 - 8 1/4	1
16	DOOR PULL	TO SUIT	1
17	LOCKING ARM	TO SUIT	1
18	COTTER PIN	1 1/8 LONG	4
19	DOOR STOP	1/4 SQ. X 9 1/4 LG.	1

DRILL FOR PART NO 18

EXPLODED VIEW

As you study the plans, also try to visualize *how* the project will be assembled. Note which parts you will put together first, second, and so on—exactly how *you* will put it together.

Note: This project is mostly pinned together using the 8 pins, parts number 6.

Carefully cut all of the parts to size according to the materials list. Take care to cut all of the parts to exact size, keeping them precisely square (90 degrees). *Stop and recheck all dimensions before going on.*

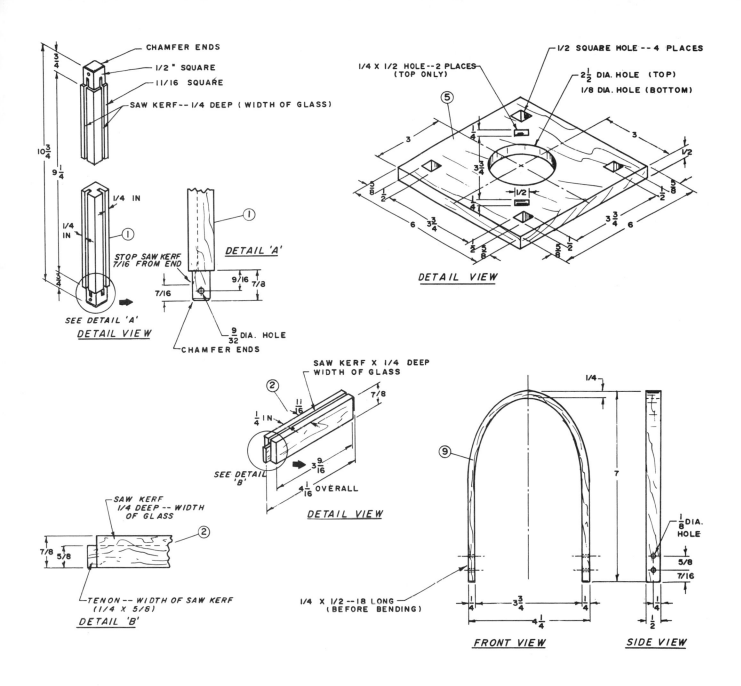

Lightly sand all surfaces and edges with medium sandpaper to remove all tool marks. Take care to keep *all* edges square and sharp.

Make each piece according to the given detail drawings. I made the pieces and fit each to the other as I went. I suggest that you cut the four ½-inch-square holes in the top and bottom pieces, parts number 5, *after* you make the other pieces. Fit the four ½-inch holes to the lantern body. I'm not exactly sure in what order the original was assembled, but I installed the glass at the same time that I assembled the pieces. It made finishing a little more difficult, but the construction was easy.

Don't forget that the top and bottom are only pinned in place.

The tin hood, part number 7, is cut out of a large "tin" juice can. After cutting it to size, bend it around some cylindrical object about 3½ inches in diameter. "Blue" it by heating it with a torch until it turns blue, and it will *look* very old. I used old carpet tacks to hold it in place.

If all parts fit together correctly, assemble the project, keeping everything square as you go. Check that all fits are tight.

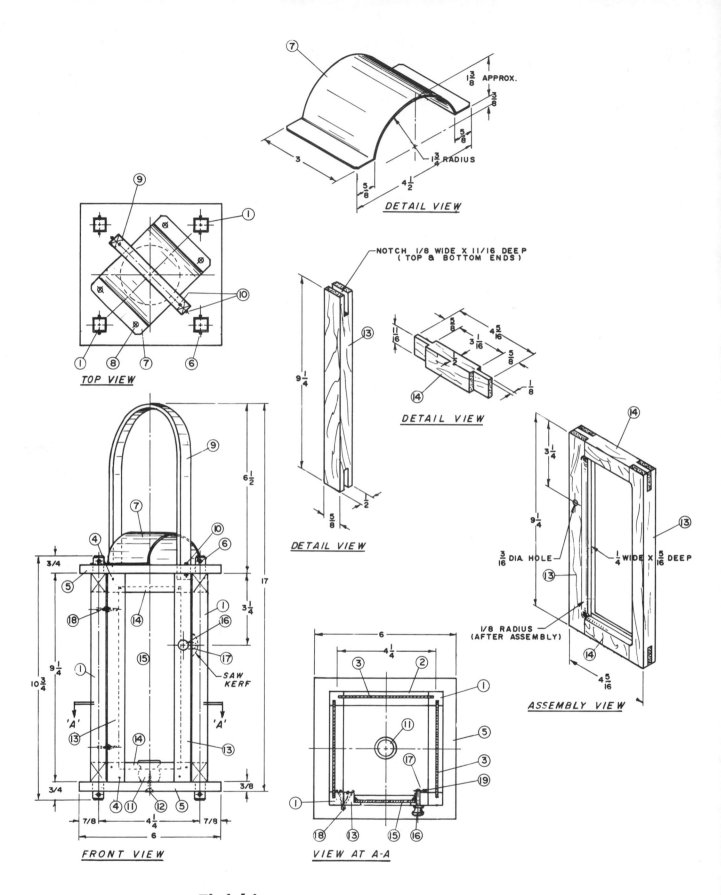

Finishing

Finish to suit, following the general finishing instructions given in the introduction.

7♦ Candle Box with Sliding Lid

The candle box with sliding lid is as popular today as it was in the days when it actually was used to store candles. I have made many of these, in all sizes for all kinds of uses. They are very handy boxes to have around the house, and they're a popular item at craft shows.

These boxes do not use much material, and there is almost *no* waste. I suggest distressing the box, and I often add a painted "crackle" finish to mine. The dimensions given are for the box pictured, but your box can be made *any* size, using whatever hardwood you have around.

Instructions

Be sure to use a straight-grained hardwood as softwood is not strong enough for the notch cutouts.

Carefully study the plans—the construction is *somewhat* unusual. Note how everything is cut from one piece of wood. The candle box pictured and shown in the plans is made from *one* board ⅜ inch thick, 6¼ inches wide, and 66 inches long. As noted, there will be almost *no* waste, with some allowance for saw kerf thickness.

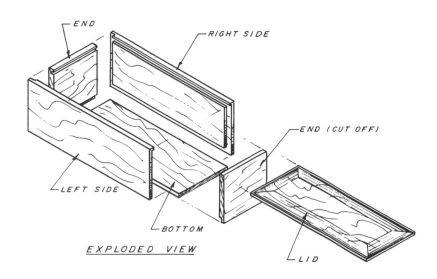

EXPLODED VIEW

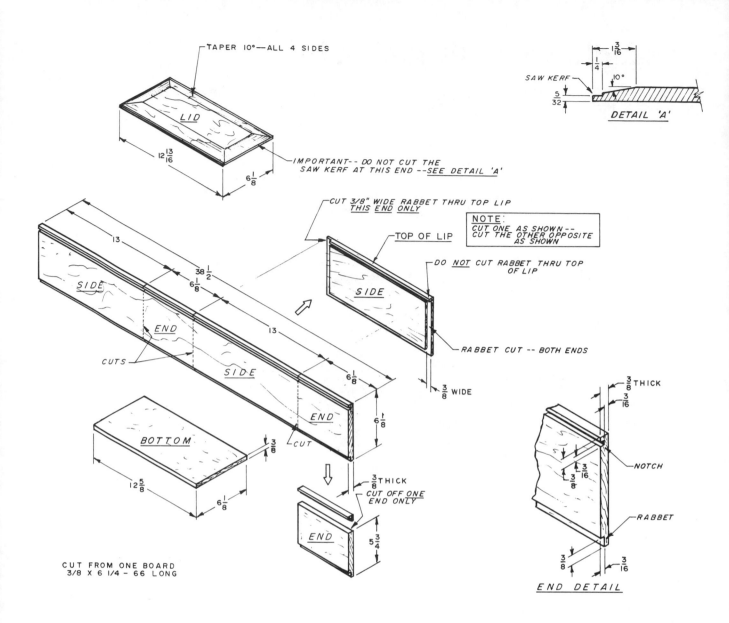

Carefully cut the lid from the board. Take care to cut each part to size, keeping the edges and corners square (90 degrees). You can cut the bottom at this time, but you might want to cut and fit the bottom to the assembly later.

On the remaining piece, cut a dado to create a notch, 3/16 inch wide by 3/16 inch deep and 3/8 inch down from the top edge, as shown in the *end detail*. Make a rabbet cut along the bottom edge, 3/8 inch wide by 3/16 inch deep, as shown in the *end detail*.

Lightly sand all surfaces and edges with medium sandpaper to remove any burrs and all tool marks. Take care to keep *all* edges square and sharp at this time.

Cut the sides and ends from the board as shown according to the given dimensions. Cut another 3/8-inch wide by 3/16-inch deep rabbet along the ends of the side pieces, taking care *not* to cut through the upper lip on one end as shown. *It is important that you make a matched pair of sides—that is, a right-hand side and a left-hand side.* On *one* of the ends, cut off a 3/8-inch-thick piece from the top edge to allow the lid to pass over and out as shown.

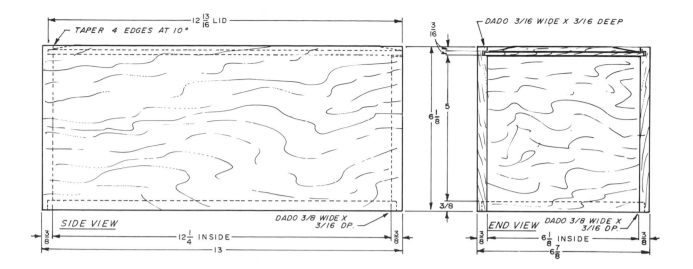

Resand all over with fine grit sandpaper, still keeping all edges sharp. Make the 10-degree bevel cuts on the four edges of the lid, as shown in *detail "A"*. Fit the lid to the notch in the box assembly.

After all pieces have been carefully made, dry-fit all of the parts—that is, put the complcte project together without glue or nails to check for accuracy and good-fitting joints. If anything needs refitting, now is the time to correct it.

Once all of the parts fit together correctly, assemble the project keeping everything square as you go. Check that all fits are tight. I usually glue the pieces together as well as fasten them with small square-cut nails. Be sure to drill small pilot holes for the nails so the wood will not split. Check that the lid slides loosely—especially if you are going to paint your box.

Finishing

Finish to suit, following the general finishing instructions in the introduction. This project can be stained or painted. If you paint your box, do not get any paint inside the notch for the lid, and try to put the paint on lightly along the area of the lid where it fits into the notch.

8 ♦ Tea Box, circa 1810

In years past *tea* was very expensive and considered a luxury. It was, therefore, locked away in tea boxes such as this one. But, what would keep a thief from simply absconding with the box itself complete with precious contents puzzles me.

Today, this tea box makes a great jewelry box—with or without the lock.

Instructions

Study the plans carefully. Note how each part is to be shaped. As you study the plans, try to *visualize* how you will make each part and then how the project will be assembled. Note the unusual joint between the box and lid. If you make it as shown, there will be a built-in lip around the inside of the box. Note which parts you will put together first, second, and so on—exactly how *you* will put them together.

Start by cutting a board ⅛ inch thick by 6³⁄₁₆ inches high and 30 inches long—see the detailed drawing of the *inside surface* of parts number 1 and 2. Choose a board that has an interesting grain pattern as it will form the front and sides of your box.

Carefully locate and cut a dado, ³⁄₁₆ inch wide by ³⁄₁₆ inch deep, exactly ⁹⁄₁₆ of an inch from the top edge *on the inside surface* of the box, as shown.

Carefully locate and cut another dado, ⅜ inch wide by ³⁄₁₆ inch deep, 1⅞ inch from the bottom edge—*again, on the inside surface* of the box, as shown.

Note: *Do not cut the last dado on the outside surface at this time.*

Cut the front, back, and two ends (parts number 1 and 2) from the prepared board. Mitre the ends at 45 degrees, but keep in mind that the dado cuts go on the *inside.* Check for a good, tight fit at all four joints— adjust as necessary. (*Tip*—save the waste piece for reference later to make the outer dado cut.)

The front, back, and ends have legs that are irregularly shaped. The patterns for the legs will have to be laid out on a ½-inch grid to make them full-size. Lay out the full-size grid on a piece of heavy paper or cardboard, and transfer the shapes to the grid, point by point.

Transfer the full-size patterns to the wood, and carefully cut out the legs on the front, back, and end pieces. Be sure to center the patterns on the wood. Check all dimensions for accuracy. Sand all over with fine grit sand-paper, keeping all edges sharp.

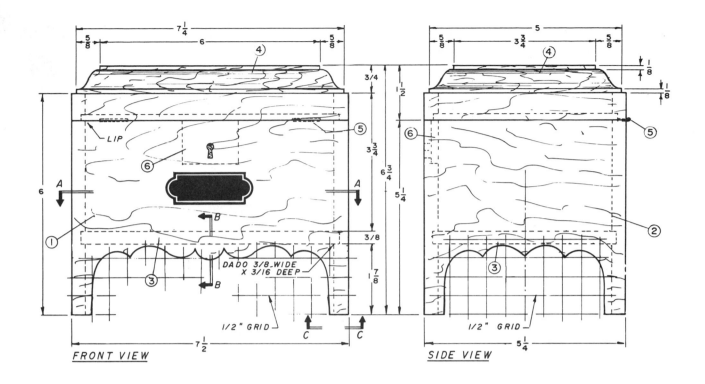

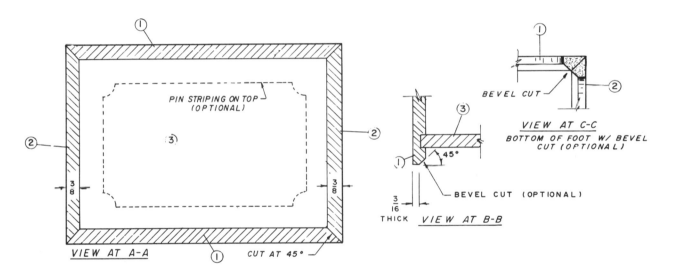

I added a step not done on the original tea box, shown at view B-B and C-C. I used a router with a 45-degree cutter and ball-bearing follower and made a 45-degree cut around the *inside* surface of the leg area. In this way my legs would *not* look as thick as they did on the original.

Carefully cut the other parts to size, fitting them to the box assembly. Take care to cut them at 90 degrees.

The top, part number 4, is cut using a router or shaper. If you do *not* have the exact same shape cutter, use what you have that is close. After it is made, no one will know yours is slightly different. As you can see in the photograph, I used a standard-size and -shape cutter that does not match the plan. The plan shows the shape of the *original* tea box.

Cut and fit the bottom, part number 3, so that it fits into the bottom dado.

Once all of the parts fit together correctly, assemble the project, keeping everything square as you go. Check that all fits are tight.

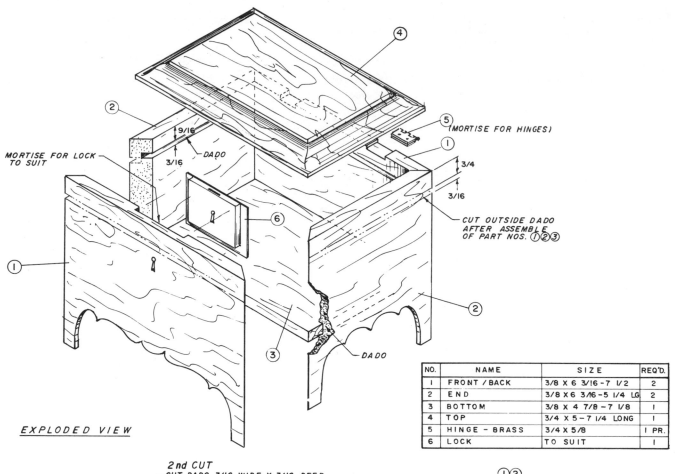

④

⑤ (MORTISE FOR HINGES)

②

9/16

MORTISE FOR LOCK
TO SUIT

DADO

3/16

①

3/4

3/16

CUT OUTSIDE DADO
AFTER ASSEMBLE
OF PART NOS. ①②③

①

⑥

②

③

DADO

EXPLODED VIEW

NO.	NAME	SIZE	REQ'D.
1	FRONT / BACK	3/8 X 6 3/16 – 7 1/2	2
2	END	3/8 X 6 3/16 – 5 1/4 LG	2
3	BOTTOM	3/8 X 4 7/8 – 7 1/8	1
4	TOP	3/4 X 5 – 7 1/4 LONG	1
5	HINGE – BRASS	3/4 X 5/8	1 PR.
6	LOCK	TO SUIT	1

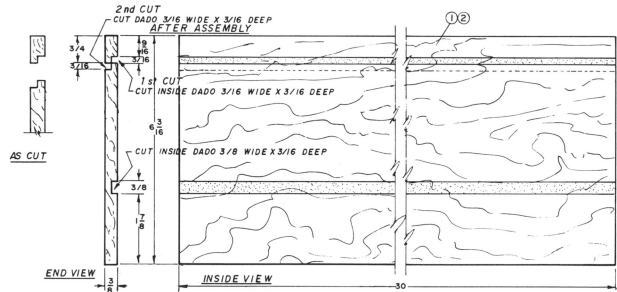

2nd CUT
CUT DADO 3/16 WIDE X 3/16 DEEP
AFTER ASSEMBLY

①②

3/4

9/16

3/16

3/16

1st CUT
CUT INSIDE DADO 3/16 WIDE X 3/16 DEEP

6 3/16

CUT INSIDE DADO 3/8 WIDE X 3/16 DEEP

AS CUT

3/8

1 7/8

END VIEW

3/8

INSIDE VIEW

30

Using the waste piece you had left over from the front, back, and ends, set your saw to make the last 3/16-inch-wide by 3/16-inch-deep dado. Cut the dado so that the *top* of the outside dado is in line with the *bottom* dado on the inside—see the end view of the detail drawing showing the board parts 1 and 2.

Attach the top, part number 4, to the box assembly—carefully centering it in place.

Finish to suit, following the general finishing instructions given in the introduction.

9♦Small Jewelry Box

I'm not sure exactly how this small chest of drawers was originally used, but it was very old. As soon as I saw it, I thought it would make a *great* jewelry box for my wife, Joyce. As you can see, it has two drawers and a storage area under the top. The drawer pulls on the original seemed a little large to me, but I made mine the same size so that the piece would be exactly like the original. If authenticity is not so important, I suggest making the drawer pulls a little smaller—perhaps a ⅝-inch or ¾-inch diameter.

Instructions

Study the plans carefully. Note how each part is to be shaped. As you study the plans, try to *visualize* how you will make each part and then how the project will be assembled. Note which parts you will put together first, second, and so on—exactly how *you* will put it together. You will be fitting drawers to the drawer openings.

The front and side skirts, parts number 9 and 10, are irregular in shape and will have to be laid out on ½-inch grids to make full-size patterns. Lay out the full-size grids on heavy paper or cardboard, and transfer the shape of each piece to the grids, point by point.

Transfer the full-size patterns to the wood, and carefully cut out the pieces. Check all dimensions for accuracy. Sand all over with fine grit sandpaper, keeping all edges sharp. Make the 45-degree mitre cuts on the ends of the skirt pieces *after* your box is assembled—make the skirt pieces fit the box.

Carefully cut the other parts to size according to the materials list. Take care to cut all of the parts to exact size, keeping them precisely square (90 degrees). *Stop and recheck all dimensions before going on.*

Make the indicated dado and rabbet cuts in the interior walls of the sides, parts number 1. Be sure to make a matched *pair*—that is, a right-hand and a left-hand side. Perhaps nothing is as disappointing as winding up with two right-hand or two left-hand sides!

Lightly sand all surfaces and edges with medium sandpaper to remove all tool marks. Take care to keep *all* edges square and sharp.

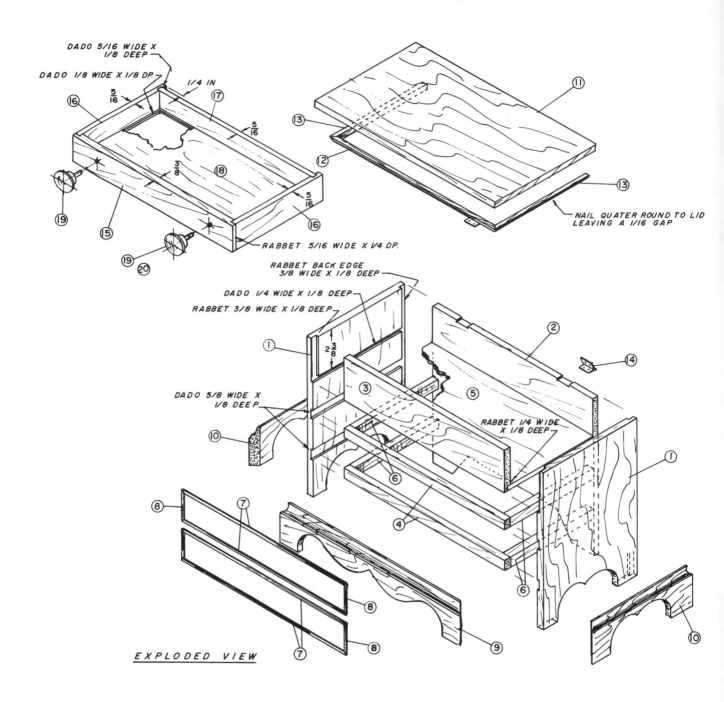

DADO 5/16 WIDE X 1/8 DEEP

DADO 1/8 WIDE X 1/8 DP.

1/4 IN

5/16

DADO 5/16 WIDE X 1/8 DEEP

DADO 1/8 WIDE X 1/8 DP.

RABBET 5/16 WIDE X 1/4 DP.

NAIL QUATER ROUND TO LID LEAVING A 1/16 GAP

RABBET BACK EDGE 3/8 WIDE X 1/8 DEEP

DADO 1/4 WIDE X 1/8 DEEP

RABBET 3/8 WIDE X 1/8 DEEP

DADO 5/8 WIDE X 1/8 DEEP

RABBET 1/4 WIDE X 1/8 DEEP

EXPLODED VIEW

I made the simple half- and quarter-round moulding, parts number 7, 8, 12, and 13, using a router with a radius cutter.

After all of the pieces have been carefully made, dry-fit the parts—that is, put the complete project together without glue or nails to check for accuracy and good-fitting joints. If anything needs refitting, now is the time to correct it.

Once all of the parts fit together correctly, assemble the project, keeping everything square as you go. Check that all fits are tight.

Attach the moulding around each of the drawer openings as shown. Take care not to get any glue on the surface of the other pieces.

Notch for the two hinges, part number 14, and add the lid, part number 11. I attached moulding to the lid, part number 11, *after* I attached the lid—this gave a very good fit.

Make the drawers as shown, fitting them to the drawer openings. Turn or purchase the drawer pulls, part number 19.

38

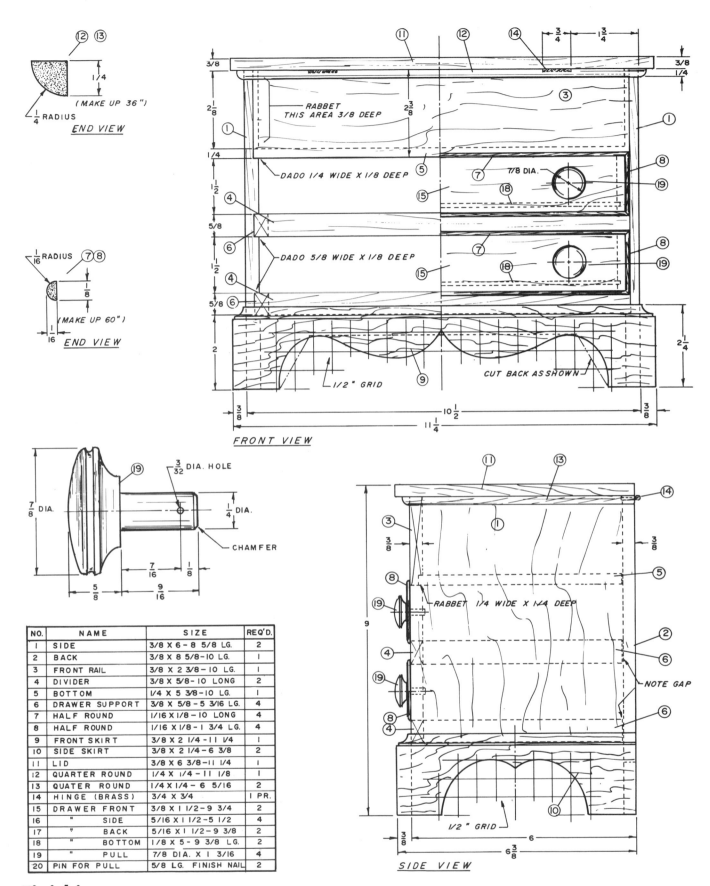

NO.	NAME	SIZE	REQ'D.
1	SIDE	3/8 X 6 - 8 5/8 LG.	2
2	BACK	3/8 X 8 5/8-10 LG.	1
3	FRONT RAIL	3/8 X 2 3/8-10 LG.	1
4	DIVIDER	3/8 X 5/8-10 LONG	2
5	BOTTOM	1/4 X 5 3/8-10 LG.	1
6	DRAWER SUPPORT	3/8 X 5/8 - 5 3/16 LG.	4
7	HALF ROUND	1/16 X 1/8-10 LONG	4
8	HALF ROUND	1/16 X 1/8 - 1 3/4 LG.	4
9	FRONT SKIRT	3/8 X 2 1/4 -11 1/4	1
10	SIDE SKIRT	3/8 X 2 1/4 - 6 3/8	2
11	LID	3/8 X 6 3/8-11 1/4	1
12	QUARTER ROUND	1/4 X 1/4 - 11 1/8	1
13	QUATER ROUND	1/4 X 1/4 - 6 5/16	2
14	HINGE (BRASS)	3/4 X 3/4	1 PR.
15	DRAWER FRONT	3/8 X 1 1/2-9 3/4	2
16	" SIDE	5/16 X 1 1/2-5 1/2	4
17	" BACK	5/16 X 1 1/2-9 3/8	2
18	" BOTTOM	1/8 X 5 - 9 3/8 LG.	2
19	" PULL	7/8 DIA. X 1 3/16	4
20	PIN FOR PULL	5/8 LG. FINISH NAIL	2

Finishing

Finish to suit, following the general finishing instructions given in the introduction.

FOLK ART AND CHILDREN'S THINGS

10 ♦ Sea Horse Weather Vane, circa 1885

Here is a very unusual weather vane pattern. It is of an original sea horse made in 1885. The original was painted red, white, and blue and was very weathered. Although it is *not* beautiful, it *is* very "different." It makes a *great* project for craft fairs. I have made three of these and, to my delight, they have sold very well.

Instructions

Study the plans carefully. Note how each part is to be shaped.

The body will have to be laid out on a ½-inch grid to make a full-size pattern. Lay out the full-size grid on heavy paper or cardboard, and transfer the shape of the body to the grid, point by point—be sure to locate the ½-inch-diameter hole on your pattern.

Transfer the full-size pattern to the wood, and carefully cut out the piece. Locate and drill for the ½-inch-diameter dowel as shown. As this is a rather simple project, you might want to consider making two or three at the same time. Simply tack two or three pieces together, and cut them all out at once.

Glue and screw the two side pieces to your project, as shown. This was the way the original one was made. I would guess that the two sides were to give the body extra strength where the ½-inch-diameter hole was drilled.

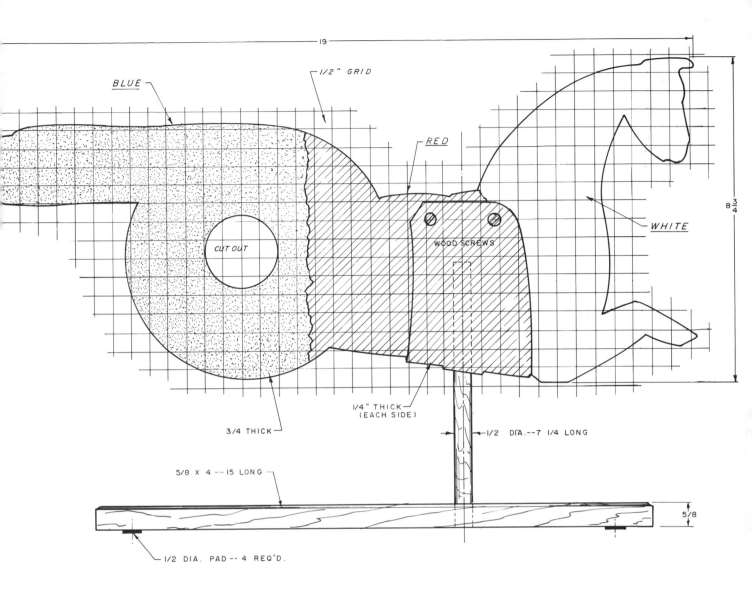

The base can be made up of most any scraps of wood you have and could be made most any size. Although it is not necessary, I suggest you use hardwood for the extra weight.

Lightly sand all surfaces and edges with medium sandpaper to remove any burrs and all tool marks. Round all edges for that "worn" look.

Finishing

Finish to suit, following the general finishing instructions given in the introduction. Be sure to give it that very "weathered" look.

To add years to your reproduction, burn it all over with a propane torch. After burning it, steel wire brush all the burnt areas down to the bare wood. The combination of burning and steel wire brushing will yield a very pleasing old look—a 150-year-old look. Thin down either latex or oil-base paint about 50 percent and paint your piece. After the paint dries, lightly steel wire brush it again, especially along the edges. Apply a light coat of a satin-top sealer. If you *really* want it to look even older, simply set it up outdoors for eight to ten months.

11 ♦ Horse Pull Toy

For the most part, the child of yesterday did not have many toys. Childhood is a fairly modern idea; in years past toys were thought to be frivolous. Life was hard and kids did not have much time to play. But one prized toy may have been some sort of pull toy like this fine example of a horse on wheels.

Instructions

Study the plans carefully. The body and legs are irregular in shape and will have to be laid out on a grid to make full-size patterns. The drawing notes a ½-inch and a 1-inch grid. Lay out the grids on heavy paper or cardboard and transfer the shape of each piece to the appropriate grid, point by point.

The wheels, parts number 7, will have to be purchased early on so that you will have them handy when you need them. If you prefer, you can make the wheels of solid wood—this would be "old"-looking also.

Carefully cut the parts according to the materials list. Take care to cut all of the parts to exact size and exactly square (90 degrees). *Stop and recheck all dimensions before going on.*

Note: The handle used has been carefully selected because it is *safe,* even though a round ball may have been used originally for the pull. *Do not use a round ball,* because it could all too easily come loose and endanger a child. The recommended handle is a 2½-inch-long piece of ½-inch-diameter dowel.

Lightly sand all surfaces and edges with medium sandpaper to remove any burrs and all tool marks. Take care to keep *all* edges square and sharp at this time.

Make all parts according to the detailed dimensions. Transfer the full-size patterns to the wood, and cut out. Check all dimensions for accuracy. Resand all over with fine grit sandpaper, still keeping all edges sharp.

Once all of the parts fit together correctly, assemble the project with glue, positioning everything as shown. Do *not* add the wheels at this time.

Note: *The feet are attached to the base, part number 5, with flathead wood screws.*

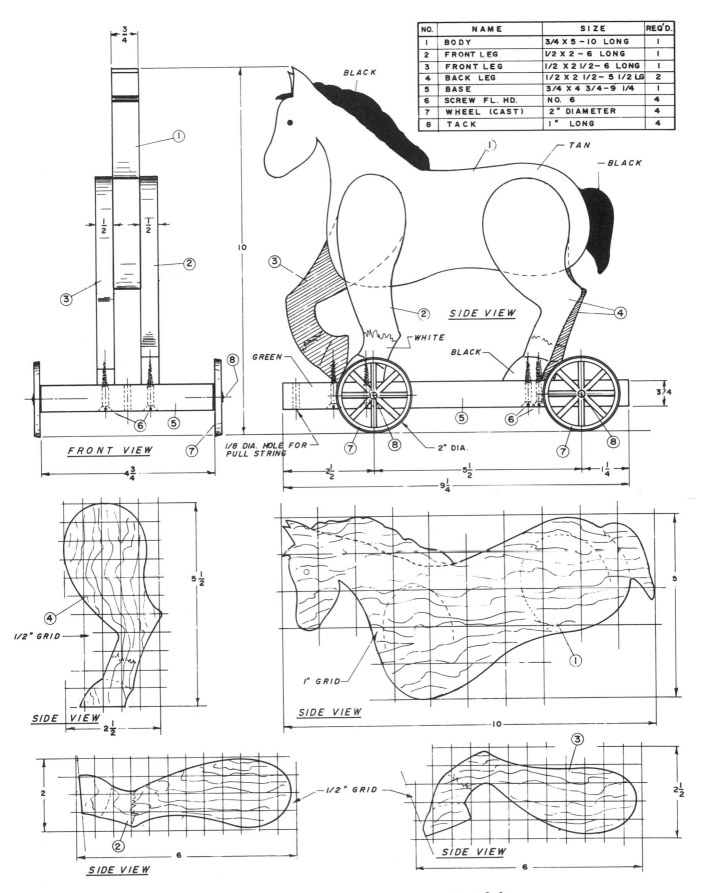

NO.	NAME	SIZE	REQ'D.
1	BODY	3/4 X 5 - 10 LONG	1
2	FRONT LEG	1/2 X 2 - 6 LONG	1
3	FRONT LEG	1/2 X 2 1/2 - 6 LONG	1
4	BACK LEG	1/2 X 2 1/2 - 5 1/2 LG	2
5	BASE	3/4 X 4 3/4 - 9 1/4	1
6	SCREW FL. HD.	NO. 6	4
7	WHEEL (CAST)	2" DIAMETER	4
8	TACK	1" LONG	4

Finish according to the drawings. Be sure to use a nontoxic paint if the
toy is intended for a child.
Attach the wheels *after* the pull toy has been painted.

43

12 ♦ Doll Chair with Dovetail Joints

Here is a small chair I saw hanging on a wall outside an antique shop in New Hope, Pennsylvania. I especially liked the dovetail joint holding the sides together. The original was painted and very "weathered." I'm not sure how this chair was originally used, but it will make a great doll's chair.

Don't worry about making the dovetail joints—they are really quite easy to make. If you have never cut a dovetail joint before, this is just the project to practice on.

Instructions

Study the plans carefully. Note how each part is to be shaped. As you study the plans, try to *visualize* how you will make each part.

The two sides, back, and brace—parts number 1, 2, and 3—are irregular in shape and will have to be laid out on ½-inch grids to make full-size patterns. Lay out the grids on heavy paper or cardboard, and transfer the shape of each piece to the appropriate grid, point by point.

Carefully cut all of the parts to overall size according to the materials list. Take care to cut all parts to exact size and exactly square (90 degrees). *Stop and recheck all dimensions before going on.*

Lightly sand all surfaces and edges with medium sandpaper to remove any burrs and all tool marks. Take care to keep *all* edges square and sharp at this time.

Transfer the full-size patterns to the wood, and cut out. Check all dimensions for accuracy. Resand all over with fine grit sandpaper, still keeping all edges sharp. It is a good idea to make the two sides, parts number 1, while they are either tacked or taped together so that you have a pair of exactly matching sides.

Carefully lay out and cut out the tail and pin of the dovetails in the side and brace pieces, parts number 1 and 3.

After all of the pieces have been carefully made, dry-fit all of the parts; that is, put the complete project together without glue or nails to check for accuracy and good-fitting joints. If anything needs refitting, now is the time to correct it.

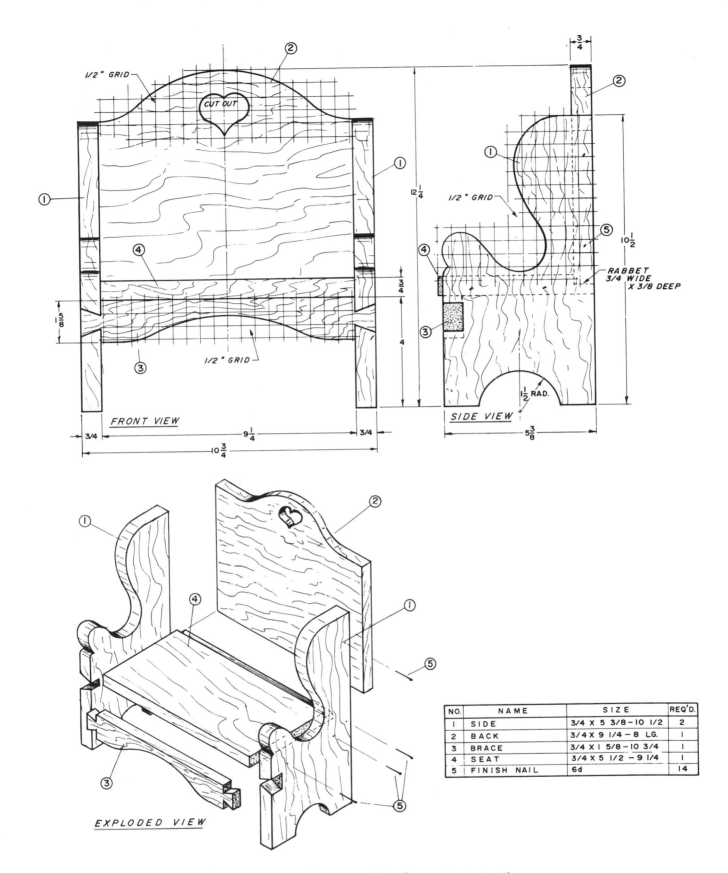

FRONT VIEW

SIDE VIEW

EXPLODED VIEW

NO.	NAME	SIZE	REQ'D.
1	SIDE	3/4 X 5 3/8 – 10 1/2	2
2	BACK	3/4 X 9 1/4 – 8 LG.	1
3	BRACE	3/4 X 1 5/8 – 10 3/4	1
4	SEAT	3/4 X 5 1/2 – 9 1/4	1
5	FINISH NAIL	6d	14

Once all of the parts fit together correctly, assemble the project starting
with the two sides and brace. Then fit the other parts to these pieces. Keep
everything square as you go. Check that all fits are tight.

Finish to suit, following the general finishing instructions given in the
introduction.

45

13 ◆ Child's Winged Rocking Chair

On chairs such as this the high back and wings were added to ward off drafts of cold air. Usually located near and facing towards the fireplace, this chair keeps the child warm and toasty, and protected on both sides from the cold.

Scale down to Doll size

Children's rockers, such as this one, are very popular with just about everyone because they are still functional, will fit into any early American decor, and add warmth to any room where they are placed.

The heart-shape cutout was a handhold so the rocker could be carried from place to place. Many children's chairs such as this one had these cut-out heart shapes.

Historically, the rocking chair is attributed to Benjamin Franklin around 1770. Children's rocking chairs, of this design, were used from around 1790 to 1825 or so.

If you collect dolls, this rocking chair, made half-size, would make an excellent way to display them.

To make the rocker *half-size*, simply use ⅜-inch-thick material, halve all dimensions, and make the layout squares ½-inch instead of 1-inch squares.

Instructions

As with any woodworking project, carefully study all of the drawings to make sure that you fully see and understand how the chair is made and put together.

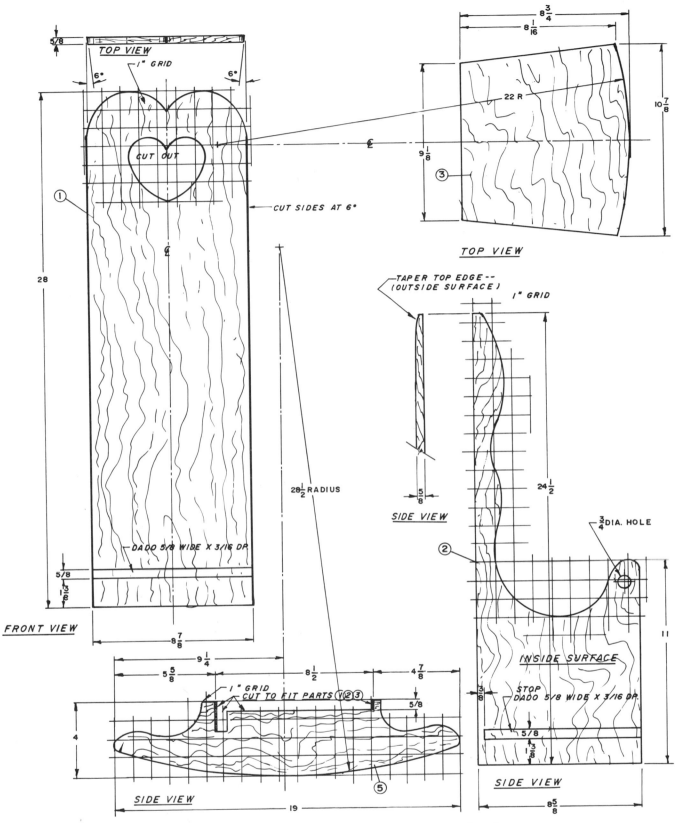

On a piece of cardboard, draw 1-inch squares and carefully transfer the shapes of the parts exactly as illustrated. Carefully cut out the patterns and transfer the shapes to the wood. Cut the dadoes, 3/16 inch deep and 5/8 inch wide, on the back, part 1, and sides, parts 2, before cutting out the outer shape. After the dadoes have been made, cut out the shape of the parts following the patterns.

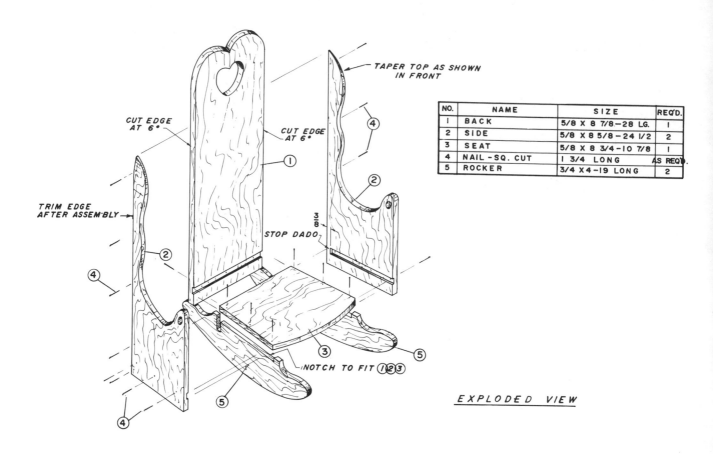

TAPER TOP AS SHOWN IN FRONT

CUT EDGE AT 6°

CUT EDGE AT 6°

TRIM EDGE AFTER ASSEMBLY

STOP DADO

$\frac{3}{8}$

NOTCH TO FIT ① ② ③

EXPLODED VIEW

NO.	NAME	SIZE	REQ'D.
1	BACK	5/8 X 8 7/8—28 LG.	1
2	SIDE	5/8 X 8 5/8—24 1/2	2
3	SEAT	5/8 X 8 3/4—10 7/8	1
4	NAIL - SQ. CUT	1 3/4 LONG	AS REQ'D.
5	ROCKER	3/4 X 4—19 LONG	2

Note: The sides, parts 2, must be a matching *pair*—one left-hand and one right-hand; be sure the dadoes are positioned correctly. Note also that the dadoes stop ⅜ inch from the back edge as shown—*see* the plans.

Cut the seat, part 3, as shown, taking care that the grain is going the correct direction and that you hold the 10⅞-inch dimension as shown. Cut or plane the six-degree angle into the back, part 1, as shown.

Cut and sand the rockers, parts number 5, as a *pair*, taking care that the 28½-inch-radius arc is continuous and does *not* have any flat spots in its entire length. Mark the front end of the rockers for identification, as the front end is slightly different than the back end. The pieces must be assembled with fronts facing the front of the rocker. You might want to cut out the top notch *after* you assemble the back, sides, and seat so that you will have a good, tight fit.

Dry-fit all of the parts to check that they all fit and go together correctly.

The back, part 1, and the sides, parts 2, should fit exactly into the seat, part 3. Trim as necessary to ensure a tight fit. The sides, parts 2, should fit into the six-degree cut into the back, part 1, and the rabbets in these parts should fit nicely into the seat, part 3. Glue and nail together, once everything fits correctly.

Add the rockers, parts 5, along the sides of the seat, part 3. Glue and nail the assembly together taking care that the two fronts of the rockers are facing towards the front of the seat and parallel to the side edges of the seat.

After assembly, sand all over. Distress lightly to suit as you wish, and stain with a stain of your choice. Apply two or three coats of satin-finish tung oil. After this has thoroughly dried, steel-wool the entire rocker with 0000 steel wool. Apply a coat of paste wax, and your project is complete, ready to enjoy for years to come.

14 ◆ Hooded Doll Cradle

Years ago, almost everyone believed that night air promoted lung disorders. Cradles, such as this one, therefore, were made with solid sides, side wings, and hoods in order to ward off those dangerous drafts of the night. Full-size cradles were made as far back as 1660, but most of the ones we see today are from the 1800s. It is unusual to find a small doll cradle such as this one.

This hooded doll rocker is fun to make and will provide countless hours of play and a place for your daughter or granddaughter to put her favorite doll to sleep at night.

The cradle has simple flowing lines and follows the traditional lines of cradles made around the turn of the twentieth century. This one was made in the New England area of pine. Some were made of poplar, and many were painted.

This model rocks from side to side as was most common. However, some people of the time thought that rockers should be positioned lengthwise to deter colic. Although rockers had been used on cradles throughout the world, it was three or four hundred years before anyone thought to add rockers to adults' chairs.

Instructions

As with any woodworking project, carefully study all of the drawings to make sure that you fully see and understand how the cradle is made and put together.

I used regular No. 2 knotty pine for the cradle I made, but if I make another, I will be sure to use knot-free, No. 1 pine—I think it looks better. Note that the sides of the original cradle I copied were made in two pieces, so I made mine in two pieces. If you wish to eliminate a step, use one 9½-inch-wide piece of wood in place of glueing up two pieces as I did. If you have a biscuit joiner, use biscuits in place of the three dowels, parts number 4C, as shown.

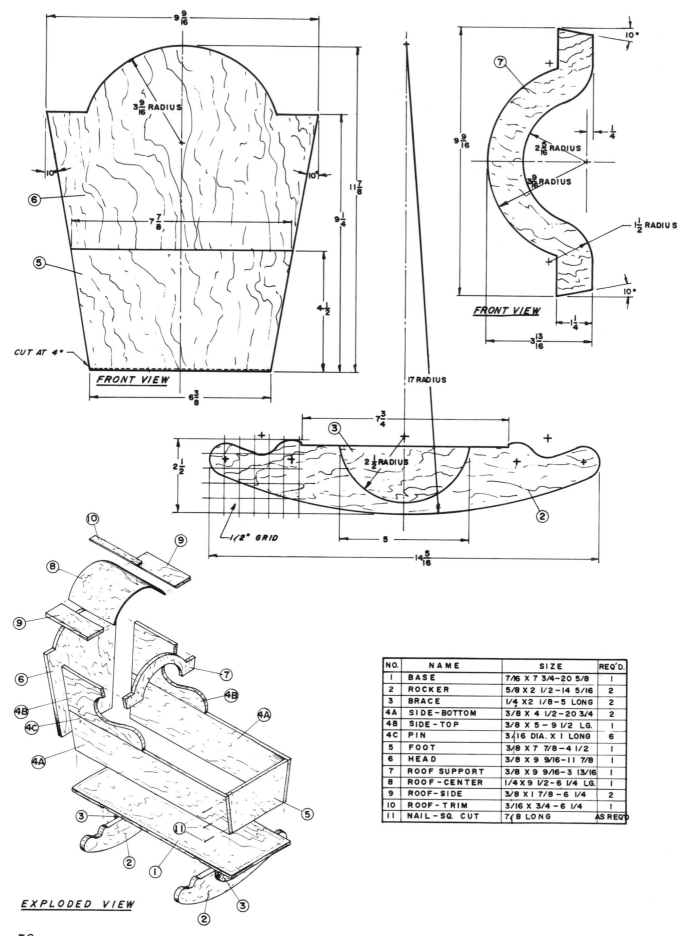

FRONT VIEW

9 9/16

3 9/16 RADIUS

10° 10°

7 7/8

11 7/8

9 1/4

4 1/2

CUT AT 4°

6 3/8

FRONT VIEW

⑥ ⑤

7

10°

9 9/16

2 5/8 RADIUS

1/4

3 9/16 RADIUS

1 1/2 RADIUS

10°

3 13/16

1 1/4

17 RADIUS

7 3/4

2 1/2

2 1/2 RADIUS

1/2" GRID

5

14 5/16

③ ②

EXPLODED VIEW

⑩ ⑨ ⑧ ⑨ ⑥ ④B ④B ④C ④A ④A ⑦ ④B ⑤ ③ ⑪ ③ ② ① ②

NO.	NAME	SIZE	REQ'D.
I	BASE	7/16 X 7 3/4 - 20 5/8	I
2	ROCKER	5/8 X 2 1/2 - 14 5/16	2
3	BRACE	1/4 X 2 1/8 - 5 LONG	2
4A	SIDE - BOTTOM	3/8 X 4 1/2 - 20 3/4	2
4B	SIDE - TOP	3/8 X 5 - 9 1/2 LG.	I
4C	PIN	3/16 DIA. X I LONG	6
5	FOOT	3/8 X 7 7/8 - 4 1/2	I
6	HEAD	3/8 X 9 9/16 - 11 7/8	I
7	ROOF SUPPORT	3/8 X 9 9/16 - 3 13/16	I
8	ROOF - CENTER	1/4 X 9 1/2 - 6 1/4 LG.	I
9	ROOF - SIDE	3/8 X I 1/8 - 6 1/4	2
10	ROOF - TRIM	3/16 X 3/4 - 6 1/4	I
11	NAIL - SQ. CUT	7/8 LONG	AS REQ'D

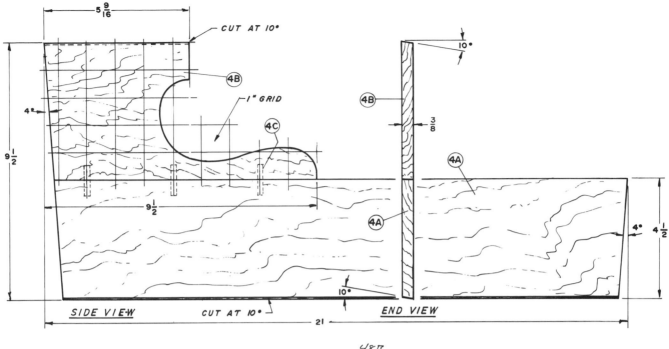

SIDE VIEW   CUT AT 10°   END VIEW

Cut all of the pieces to size according to the materials list. If you do not have a planer you will have to have the stock custom-planed to the required ⅜-inch thickness. Perhaps you can have this done at a local high school wood shop.

Lay out full-size patterns for the sides, parts number 4A and 4B, the rocker, part number 2, and the roof support, part number 7. Transfer these patterns to the wood, and cut out the pieces.

Carefully lay out the foot and head, parts number 5 and 6, according to the given dimensions. Be sure the bottom areas of both are exactly the same shape. The drawing shows the two pieces drawn on top of each other. Cut the bottom edges of both at 4 degrees, as shown.

Note: The top and bottom edges of the assembled sides, parts number 4A, 4B, and 4C, are cut at 10 degrees. *Important: Be sure to make one right-hand and one left-hand side.*

Assemble the two sides, parts number 4, to the foot, part number 5, and head, part number 6. Plane and/or sand the bottom for the assembly so that you have a *flat* surface along the bottom edges.

Attach the rockers, parts number 2 and 3, to the bottom board, part number 1, about 11⅜ inch apart, as shown on the plans. Add the bottom assembly to the side, foot, and head assembly.

Assemble the cradle with glue and square-cut nails, keeping everything "square" and tight. Take care not to get glue on exposed surfaces, and wipe off any excess glue immediately.

Attach the roof support, part number 7, to the cradle assembly. Glue and clamp the center roof, part number 8, in place. I made a series of parallel saw kerfs about ⅛ inch apart on the *inside* surface to make the bending easier. **Note:** The original cradle did *not* have these saw kerfs—the maker probably steam-bent its top. You can either steam-bend the top or make the saw kerfs as you prefer.

After the glue sets, add the two roof sides, parts number 9. Lastly, add the roof trim, part number 10—this should hold the roof assembly in place nicely.

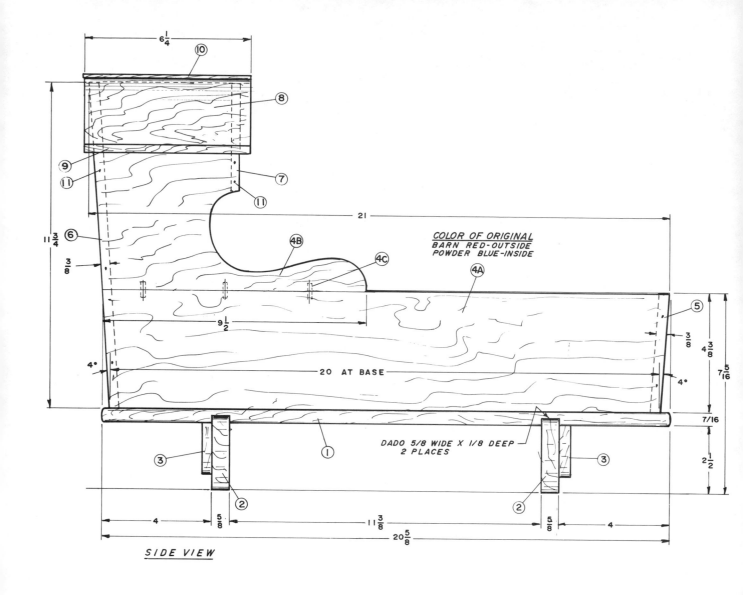

SIDE VIEW

Finishing

After assembly, sand all over; distress lightly—remember, your reproduction should look 150 years old. The original cradle was painted a light powder blue inside and barn red outside. This makes a nice combination. I used a latex blue on the inside, adding 50 percent water to the paint for a light wash-coat effect. Undiluted latex paint was used for the outside. After the paints dry, sand over with fine sandpaper; try to sand through the edges slightly where there would normally be "wear." Steel-wool the entire cradle, inside and out, with 0000 steel wool. Apply a top coat of light walnut stain over the paint—this will really add "years" to your cradle.

Apply a coat of paste wax, and complete the project by adding one tired doll.

15 ◆ Rocking Horse

Having a grandchild, I just *had* to make a rocking horse. I looked for an original horse that looked old, that was functional, and that would be fun to ride. I found this one in Maine and thought it would fit the bill. However, as I write my grandson is only 9 months old, so I will have to wait a year or two to see if I was right in my choice or not. The horse is easy to make as the body is simply attached to a frame. The only difficult part was making the rectangular holes in the rockers, parts number 8, for the foot rest, part number 9.

Instructions

Study the plans carefully. Note how each part is to be shaped. As you study the plans, try to *visualize* how you will make each part and how the project will be assembled. Note which parts you will put together first, second, and so on. Notice that the body and/or rocker is simply attached to a frame made up of the seat, front, and sides, parts number 1, 2, and 3.

Carefully lay out and make the seat, part number 1, following the given dimensions. Locate and cut the dadoes at the given angles.

Make the front and sides, parts number 2 and 3, and assemble these parts to make up the frame assembly.

The two seat front and back pieces, parts number 5, the head, part number 6, and the rockers, parts number 8, are irregular in shape and will each have to be laid out on a ½-inch or 1-inch grid, as noted, to make a full-size pattern. Lay out a full-size grid on heavy paper or cardboard, and transfer the shape of each piece to the appropriate grid, point by point.

Transfer the full-size patterns to the wood, and carefully cut out the pieces. Check all of the dimensions for accuracy. Sand all over with fine grit paper, keeping all edges sharp. Note that the head, part number 6, is made up of two pieces of ¾-inch-thick wood glued together before cutting.

Locate, but do not cut out, the rectangular ¾-inch by 4¼-inch hole for the foot rest at this time—it has to be cut at two odd angles.

Lightly sand all surfaces and edges with medium sandpaper to remove all tool marks. Take care to keep *all* edges square and sharp.

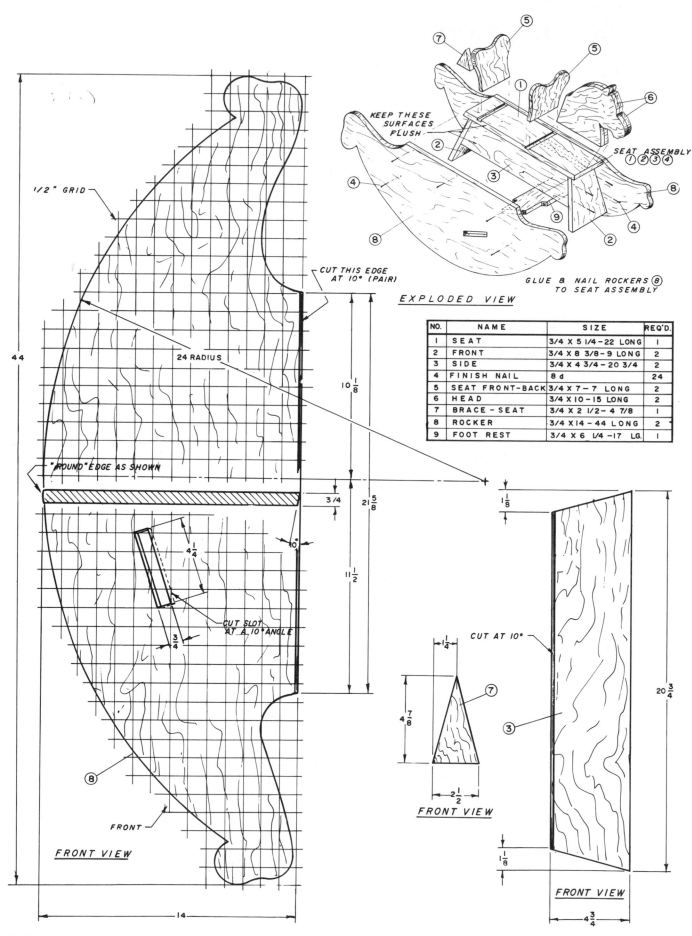

KEEP THESE
SURFACES
FLUSH

SEAT ASSEMBLY
① ② ③ ④

EXPLODED VIEW

GLUE & NAIL ROCKERS ⑧
TO SEAT ASSEMBLY

NO.	NAME	SIZE	REQ'D.
I	SEAT	3/4 X 5 1/4 - 22 LONG	I
2	FRONT	3/4 X 8 3/8 - 9 LONG	2
3	SIDE	3/4 X 4 3/4 - 20 3/4	2
4	FINISH NAIL	8 d	24
5	SEAT FRONT-BACK	3/4 X 7 - 7 LONG	2
6	HEAD	3/4 X 10 - 15 LONG	2
7	BRACE - SEAT	3/4 X 2 1/2 - 4 7/8	I
8	ROCKER	3/4 X 14 - 44 LONG	2
9	FOOT REST	3/4 X 6 1/4 - 17 LG.	I

1/2" GRID

CUT THIS EDGE
AT 10° (PAIR)

24 RADIUS

10 1/8

"ROUND" EDGE AS SHOWN

3/4

21 5/8

10°

44

11 1/2

4 1/4

3/4

CUT SLOT
AT A 10° ANGLE

⑧

FRONT

FRONT VIEW

14

1 1/8

CUT AT 10°

1 1/4

4 7/8

⑦

2 1/2

FRONT VIEW

③

20 3/4

1 1/8

FRONT VIEW

4 3/4

54

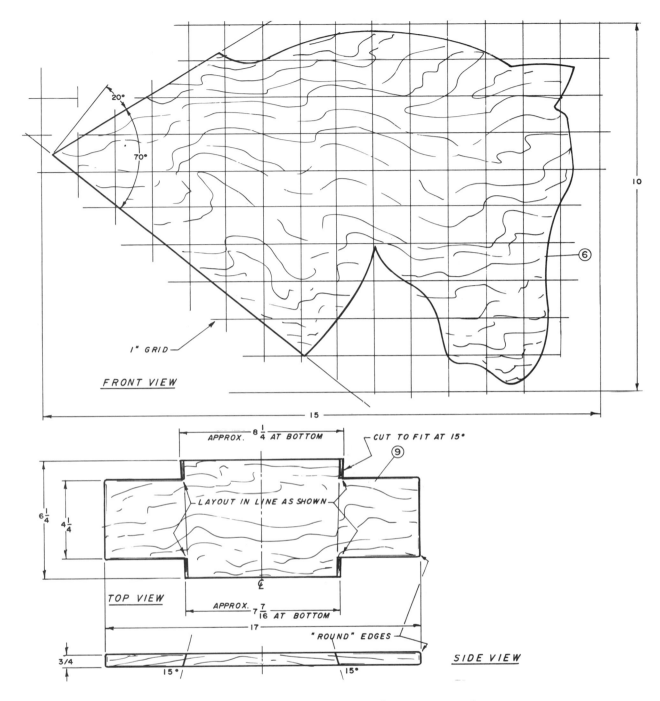

FRONT VIEW

1" GRID

20°
70°
10
15
⑥

TOP VIEW

APPROX. 8 1/4 AT BOTTOM
CUT TO FIT AT 15°
⑨
LAYOUT IN LINE AS SHOWN
6 1/4
4 1/4
℄
APPROX. 7 7/16 AT BOTTOM
17
"ROUND" EDGES

SIDE VIEW

3/4
15°
15°

Note: The dimensions given for the foot rest, part number 9, *are only approximate.* It is best to fit the foot rest to the sides at assembly.

After all pieces have been carefully made, dry-fit all of the parts. If anything needs refitting, now is the time to correct it. Temporarily tack the two rockers, parts number 8, to the body assembly exactly where they should be. With the two rockers in place, drill a series of ¾-inch-diameter holes where you located the opening for the foot rest. *Important: Hold the drill parallel to the floor and at 90 degrees to the seat board.* Using a wood chisel, chisel the ¾-inch-wide by 4¼-inch rectangular hole for the foot rest. Note that this means the rectangular hole is cut at very odd angles to the rocker design.

Make the foot rest, part number 9, using the given dimension to get you close to the size, but fit it to the rectangular holes with the rockers in place. This is the only tricky part of the project.

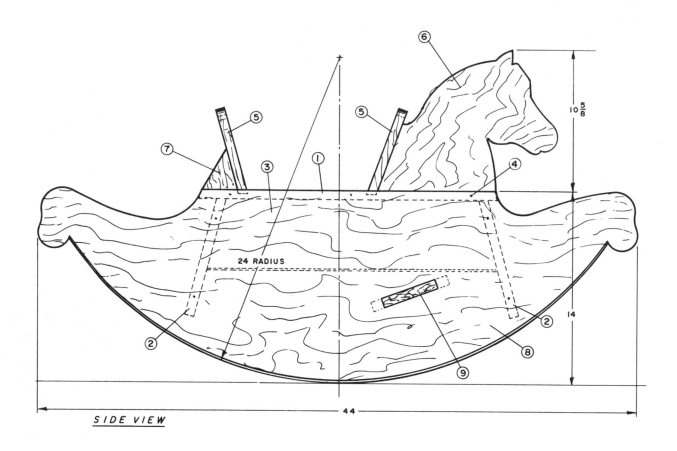

24 RADIUS

14

10 5/8

44

SIDE VIEW

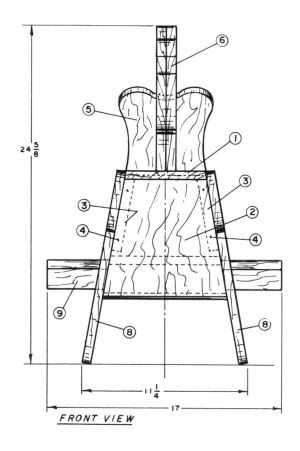

24 5/8

11 1/4

17

FRONT VIEW

56

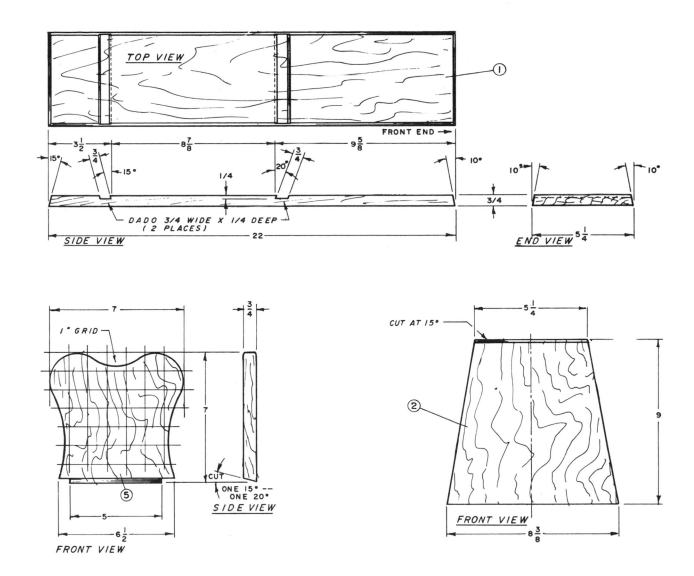

Once all of the parts fit together correctly, assemble the project keeping everything square as you go. Check that all fits are tight. Don't forget to add the seat brace, part number 7, behind the seat back. This piece might have to be adjusted slightly so that you get sufficiently tight joints.

Reminder: Be sure to add the foot rest before you attach the rockers to the body assembly. This may seem too obvious to mention after all the fitting and cutting, but *I* almost forgot it.

Finishing

Finish to suit, following the general finishing instructions given in the introduction. The original was made of pine and stained.

SIMPLE WALL BOXES

16♦Small Wall Box

Here is a small wall box that I thought was very interesting and unusual. I don't know *what* it was used for—the design even seems a bit top-heavy. This is what the original looked like, so here it is! I found this one in northern Vermont, near Burlington. This project can be painted or stained as desired.

Instructions

Study the plans carefully. Note how each part is to be shaped. As you study the plans, try to *visualize* how you will make each part.

The back, part number 1, has an irregular shape, so it should be laid out on a ½-inch grid, as shown, to make the full-size pattern. Lay out the grid and transfer the shape of the piece to the grid, point by point.

Carefully cut all of the parts according to the materials list. Take care to cut all parts to exact size and exactly square (90 degrees).

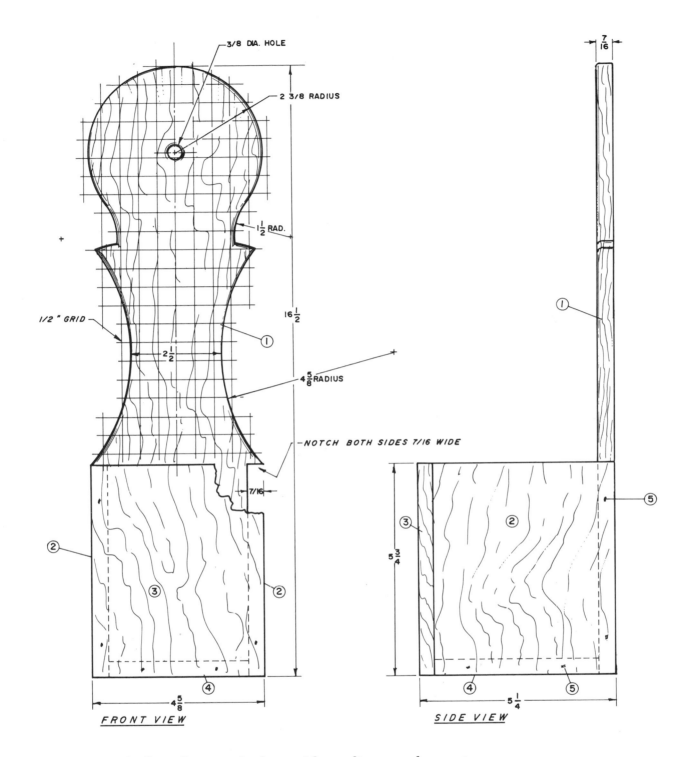

FRONT VIEW

SIDE VIEW

Lightly sand all surfaces and edges with medium sandpaper to remove any burrs and all tool marks. Take care to keep *all* edges square and sharp at this time.

Cut all of the parts following the detailed illustrations as well as the given dimensions. Check all dimensions for accuracy. Resand all over with fine grit sandpaper, still keeping all edges sharp. Take care to cut the 7/16-inch by 5¾-inch notches in the two sides of the backboard, part number 1.

After all of the pieces have been carefully made, dry-fit all parts—that is, put the complete project together without glue or nails to check for accuracy and good-fitting joints. If anything needs refitting, now is the time to correct it.

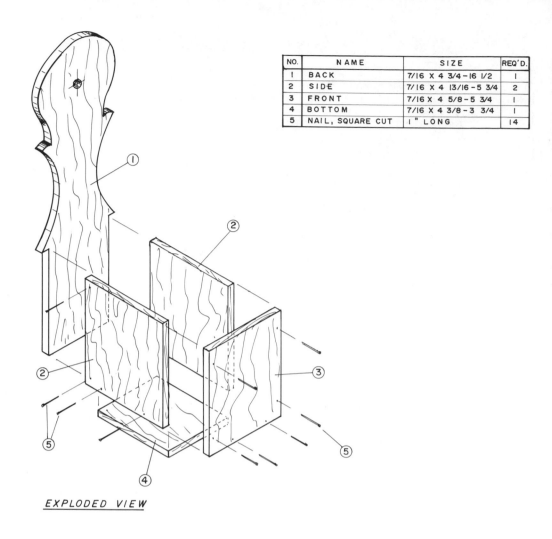

NO.	NAME	SIZE	REQ'D.
1	BACK	7/16 X 4 3/4 – 16 1/2	1
2	SIDE	7/16 X 4 13/16 – 5 3/4	2
3	FRONT	7/16 X 4 5/8 – 5 3/4	1
4	BOTTOM	7/16 X 4 3/8 – 3 3/4	1
5	NAIL, SQUARE CUT	1" LONG	14

EXPLODED VIEW

Once all of the parts fit together correctly, assemble the project, keeping everything square as you go. Check that all fits are tight. As usual, leave the square-cut nails showing—don't try to hide them; the original had them showing. "Round" all edges slightly.

Finishing

Finish to suit, following the general finishing instructions in the introduction.

17♦Long Wall Box, circa 1820

Wall boxes came in all shapes and sizes. Here is the pattern for a box made around 1820 or so someplace in New England. Its long backboard makes it somewhat different than more common examples. This wall box is especially suited for high plants or such things. The original was made of pine.

Instructions

Study the plans carefully. Note how each part is to be shaped. The backboard, part number 1, is somewhat irregular in shape; it should be laid out on a 1-inch grid to make a full-size pattern. Lay out the grid on heavy paper or cardboard, and transfer the shape of the piece to the grid, point by point. A simple pattern such as this one could be laid out directly on the wood, however.

Carefully cut the other parts according to the materials list. Take care to cut all of the parts to exact size and exactly square (90 degrees). *Stop and recheck all dimensions before going on.*

Lightly sand all surfaces and edges with medium sandpaper to remove any burrs and all tool marks. Take care to keep *all* edges square and sharp at this time.

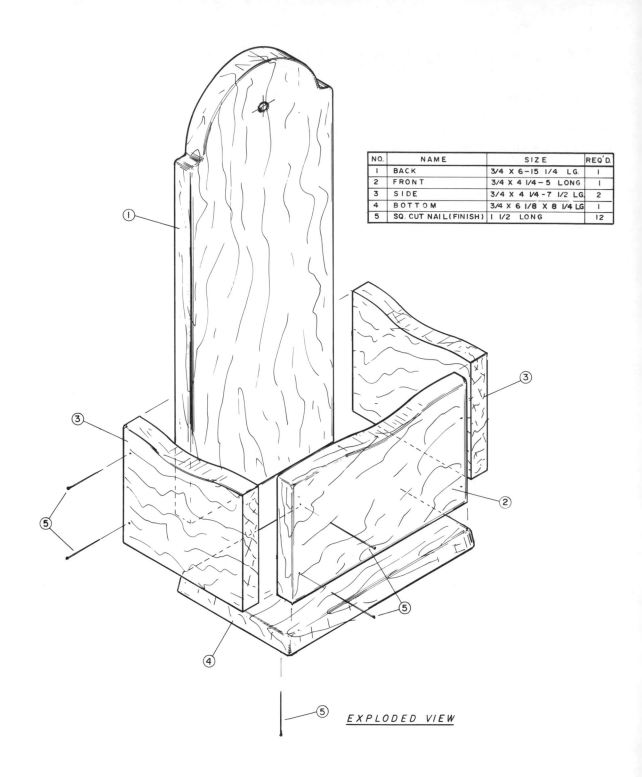

NO.	NAME	SIZE	REQ'D.
1	BACK	3/4 X 6-15 1/4 LG.	1
2	FRONT	3/4 X 4 1/4 – 5 LONG	1
3	SIDE	3/4 X 4 1/4 – 7 1/2 LG.	2
4	BOTTOM	3/4 X 6 1/8 X 8 1/4 LG	1
5	SQ. CUT NAIL(FINISH)	1 1/2 LONG	12

EXPLODED VIEW

Make all parts following the detailed illustrations and given dimensions. Full-size patterns should be transferred to the wood and cut out. Check all dimensions for accuracy. Resand all over with fine grit sandpaper, still keeping all edges sharp.

After all of the pieces have been carefully made, dry-fit the parts—that is, put the complete project together without glue or nails to check for accuracy and good-fitting joints. If anything needs refitting, now is the time to correct it.

Once all of the parts fit together correctly, assemble the project, keeping everything square as you go. Check that all fits are tight.

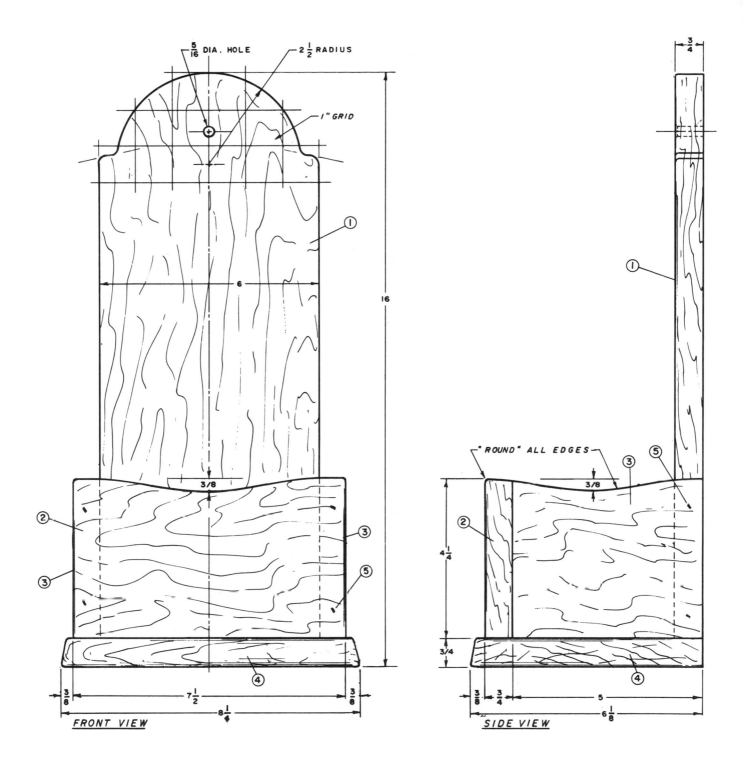

Finishing

Finish to suit, following the general finishing instructions in the introduction. This project could be stained or painted, as you prefer. The original was painted a dark blackish-green.

18♦Lollypop-Style Wall Box

The lollypop design was so popular that it is characteristic of many early American wooden pieces. The lollypop design appears two or three times in this collection of projects. In fact, project number 24 uses a *double* lollypop pattern. I have found other wall boxes very similar to this one. This one is somewhat "boxy," but is exactly as the original one was.

Instructions

Study the plans carefully. Note how each part is to be shaped. The backboard, part number 1, is somewhat irregular in shape; it should be laid out on a 1-inch grid to make a full-size pattern.

Lay out the grid on heavy paper or cardboard, and transfer the shape of the piece to the grid, point by point. A simple pattern such as this one could be laid out directly on the wood, however.

Carefully cut all other parts according to the materials list. Take care to cut all of the parts to exact size and exactly square (90 degrees). *Stop and recheck all dimensions before going on.*

Lightly sand all surfaces and edges with medium sandpaper to remove any burrs and all tool marks. Take care to keep *all* edges square and sharp at this time.

Make all parts following the detailed illustrations and given dimensions. Check all dimensions for accuracy. Resand all over with fine grit sandpaper, still keeping all edges sharp.

After all of the pieces have been carefully made, dry-fit all of the parts—that is, put the complete project together without glue or nails to check for accuracy and good-fitting joints. If anything needs refitting, now is the time to correct it.

Once all of the parts fit together correctly, assemble the project, keeping everything square as you go. Check that all fits are tight.

"Round" all edges to simulate years of wear, and distress all over.

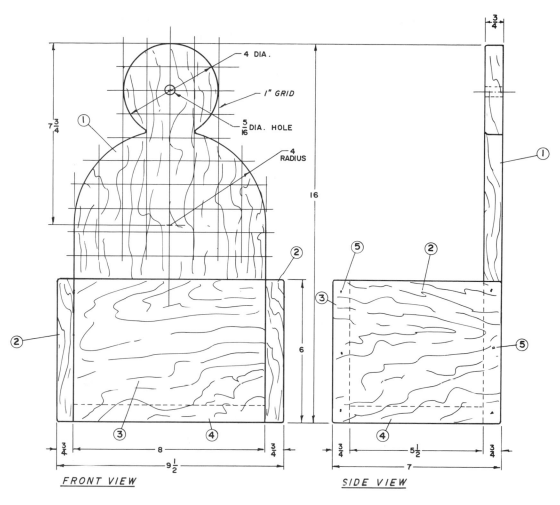

4 DIA.

1" GRID

$\frac{5}{16}$ DIA. HOLE

4 RADIUS

$7\frac{3}{4}$

16

6

$\frac{3}{4}$ 8 $\frac{3}{4}$

$9\frac{1}{2}$

FRONT VIEW

$\frac{3}{4}$

$\frac{3}{4}$ $5\frac{1}{2}$ $\frac{3}{4}$

7

SIDE VIEW

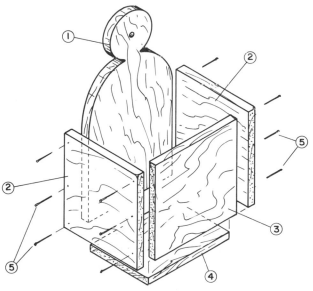

EXPLODED VIEW

NO.	NAME	SIZE	REQ'D.
1	BACK	3/4 X 8 - 16 LONG	1
2	SIDE	3/4 X 6 - 7 LONG	2
3	FRONT	3/4 X 6 - 8 LONG	1
4	BOTTOM	3/4 X 5 1/2 - 8 LG.	1
5	FINISH NAIL	6 d	12

Finishing

Finish to suit, following the general finishing instructions in the introduction. This project can be stained or painted, but be sure to distress it so that it looks very old.

19♦New Hampshire Wall Box

The design of this simple wall box is a "takeoff" of a lollypop top, similar to project 18. It has an unusual step below the round lollypop top. The box is a little "heavy"—that is, thick—but still it is a nice old wall box, which I found in southern New Hampshire.

Instructions

Study the plans carefully. Note how each part is made and shaped. The backboard, part number 1, has an irregular shape; it will have to be laid out on a 1-inch grid to make a full-size pattern. Lay out a grid on heavy paper or cardboard, and transfer the shape of the piece to the grid, point by point, as shown.

Note: The backboard, part number 1, has a ¾-inch by 4-inch notch for the sides, parts number 3—*see* the exploded view.

Carefully cut out the remaining parts according to the materials list. Take care to cut all parts to exact size and exactly square (90 degrees). *Stop and recheck all dimensions before going on.*

Lightly sand all surfaces and edges with medium sandpaper to remove any burrs and all tool marks. Take care to keep *all* edges square and sharp at this time.

After all pieces have been carefully made, dry-fit all of the parts—that is, put the complete project together without glue or nails to check for accuracy and good-fitting joints. If anything needs refitting, now is the time to correct it.

Once all of the parts fit together correctly, assemble the project using glue and square-cut nails, keeping everything square. Check that all fits are tight.

"Round" all edges that would have normally been worn through the years.

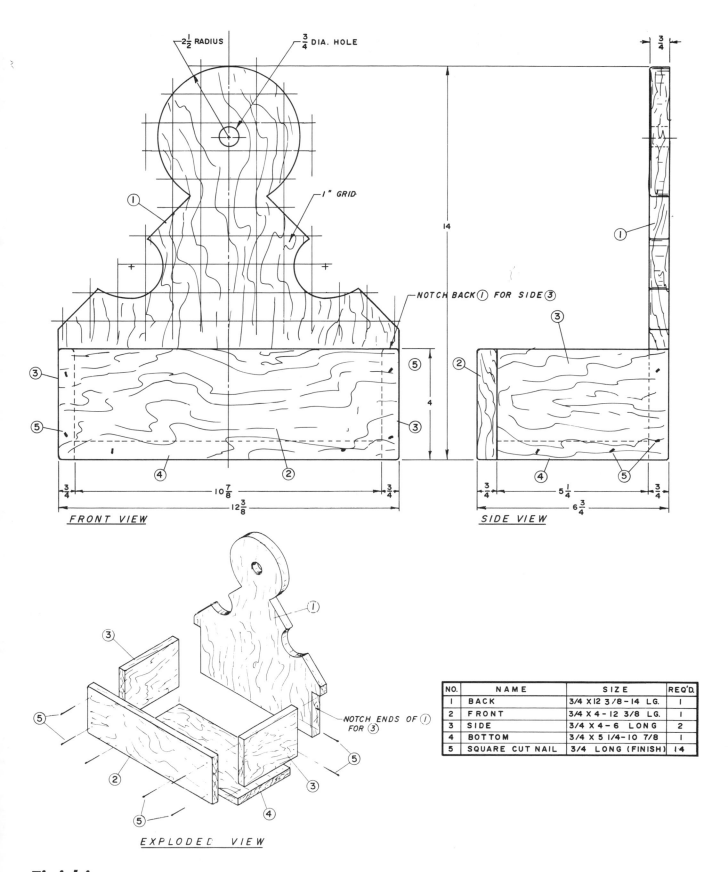

NO.	NAME	SIZE	REQ'D.
I	BACK	3/4 X 12 3/8 - 14 LG.	I
2	FRONT	3/4 X 4 - 12 3/8 LG.	I
3	SIDE	3/4 X 4 - 6 LONG	2
4	BOTTOM	3/4 X 5 1/4 - 10 7/8	I
5	SQUARE CUT NAIL	3/4 LONG (FINISH)	14

Finishing

Finish to suit, following the general finishing instructions in the introduction. This project can be either stained or painted—if you use paint, try crackling; this project is particularly suitable for applying a crackle finish.

20 ♦ Wall Box with Heart-Shape Design

Cutout heart-shape designs seem as popular today as they were in years past. Here are the plans for a wall box with an original heart cutout that is very easy to make. It has an unusual feature—notice how the sides are trimmed on an angle at the top area to blend into the backboard shape. I don't recall seeing many wall boxes with "shoulders" such as these—which is why I copied and recorded this one.

Instructions

Study the plans carefully. Note how each part is to be shaped and *how* you will make each part with the tools you have.

The backboard, part number 1, and the two sides, parts number 2, are irregular in shape and will have to be laid out on a ½-inch grid to make full-size patterns. Lay out the grids on heavy paper or cardboard and transfer the shape of each piece to the appropriate grid, point by point—don't forget the pattern for the heart.

Cut out the backboard following the plans. Locate and cut out the heart shape following the plans for the front piece, part number 3. On heart cutouts such as this one, I usually drill two holes to form the top part of the heart. Doing this ensures two perfect radii around the top half of the heart. I recommend drilling two ⅞-inch-diameter holes, ¾ inch apart as shown—this will complete half of the heart cutout.

To make a perfect pair of sides, parts number 2, tape or tack the two sides together and cut them out at the same time. Don't forget to make the ½-inch by 4⅝-inch notch for the front, part number 3.

Cut the bottomboard, part number 4, following the given dimensions. Take care to cut it at exactly 90 degrees and to fit the bottom opening. *Stop and recheck all dimensions before going on.*

Lightly sand all surfaces and edges with medium sandpaper to remove any burrs and all tool marks. Take care to keep *all* edges square and sharp *except* the heart cutout. "Round" the outer edge of the heart at this time.

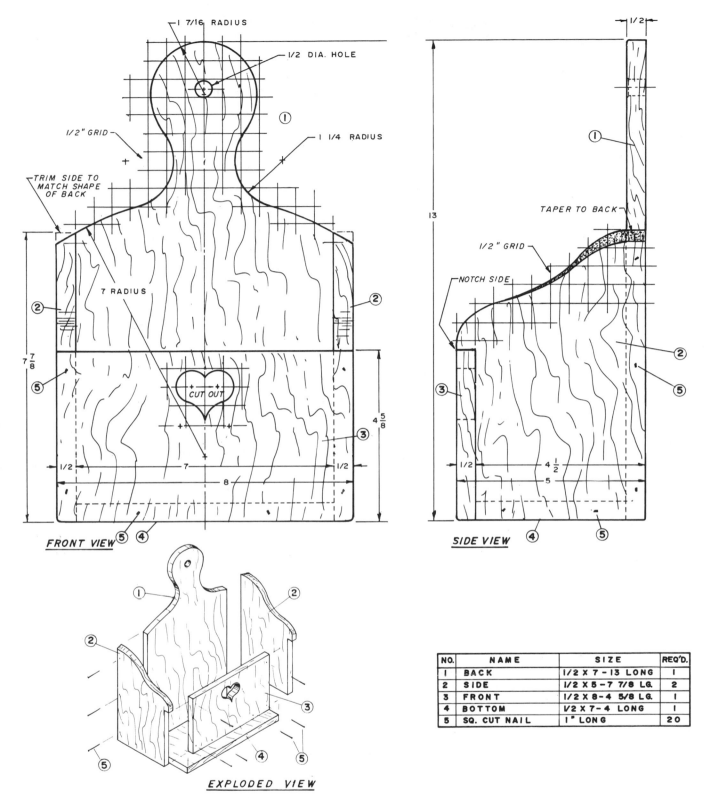

FRONT VIEW

SIDE VIEW

EXPLODED VIEW

NO.	NAME	SIZE	REQ'D.
1	BACK	1/2 X 7 - 13 LONG	1
2	SIDE	1/2 X 5 - 7 7/8 LG.	2
3	FRONT	1/2 X 8 - 4 5/8 LG.	1
4	BOTTOM	1/2 X 7 - 4 LONG	1
5	SQ. CUT NAIL	1" LONG	20

After all of the pieces have been carefully made, dry-fit the parts—that is, put the complete project together without glue or nails to check for accuracy and good-fitting joints. If anything needs refitting, now is the time to correct it.

Once all of the parts fit together correctly, assemble the project keeping everything square as you go. Check that all fits are tight.

Finish to suit, following the general finishing instructions in the introduction.

21♦Wall Candle Box

This is a *great* wall box—it is unusual, easy to make, and very functional. I found this one *years* ago, took several photographs and, as usual, noted carefully the overall dimensions and patterns. It has been so long that I do not remember where I came across this one. This project is particularly suited to practicing your "crackle"-painting finish on.

Instructions

Study the plans carefully. Notice how each part is to be made.

The back, part number 1, is the only irregularly shaped part and should be laid out on a 1-inch grid to make a full-size pattern. Lay out a grid on heavy paper or cardboard, and transfer the shape of the piece to the grid, point by point—don't forget to locate the 5/8-inch-diameter hole.

Carefully cut all of the parts according to the materials list. Take care to cut all parts to exact size and exactly square (90 degrees). *Stop and recheck all dimensions before going on.*

Lightly sand all surfaces and edges with medium sandpaper to remove any burrs and all tool marks. Take care to keep *all* edges square and sharp at this time.

Cut out all parts following the detailed dimensions. Transfer the full-size patterns to the wood and cut out the pieces. Check all dimensions for accuracy. Resand all over with fine grit sandpaper, still keeping all edges sharp.

After all of the pieces have been carefully made, dry-fit the parts—that is, put the complete project together without glue or nails to check for accuracy and good-fitting joints. If anything needs refitting, now is the time to correct it.

Once all of the parts fit together correctly, assemble the project keeping everything square as you go. Check that all fits are tight.

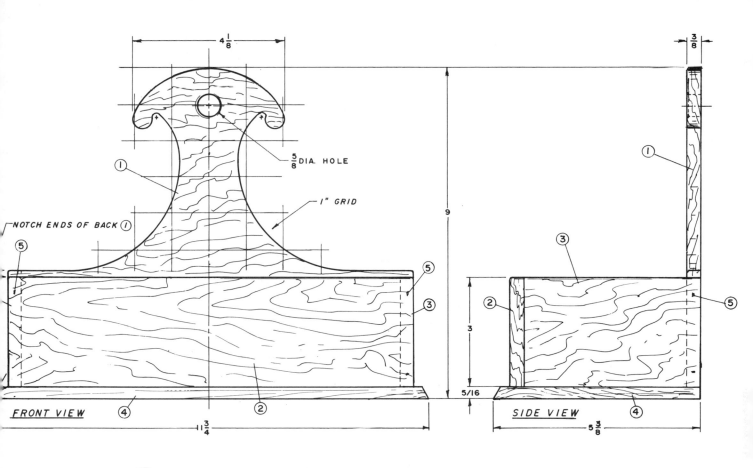

4 1/8

⅝ DIA. HOLE

1" GRID

NOTCH ENDS OF BACK ①

9

3/8

FRONT VIEW

3

5/16

11 3/4

SIDE VIEW

5 3/8

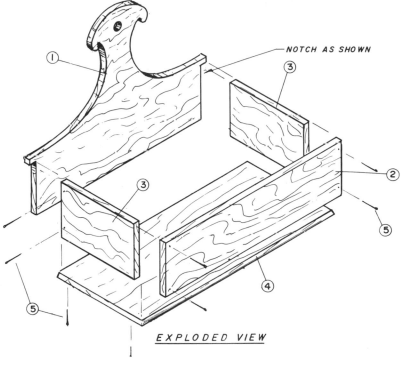

NOTCH AS SHOWN

EXPLODED VIEW

NO.	NAME	SIZE	REQ'D.
1	BACK	3/8 X 8 11/16 -10 1/4	1
2	FRONT	3/8 X 3 - 11 LONG	1
3	SIDE	3/8 X 3 - 4 5/8 LONG	2
4	BOTTOM	5/16 X 5 3/8 -11 3/4	1
5	SQUARE CUT NAIL	3/4 LONG (FINISH)	14

Finishing

Finish to suit, following the general finishing instructions in the introduction.

22♦Formal Queen Anne Wall Box

This is a very small, *formal* wall box. Although quite simple in construction, it has very pleasing Queen Anne lines. I recommend that you select a fine hardwood such as walnut, maple, cherry, or mahogany to make this box.

Instructions

Study the plans carefully. Note how each part is shaped, and *how* you will make each part with the tools you have.

The backboard and two sides, parts number 1 and 2, are irregular in shape; each will have to be laid out on a ½-inch grid to make full-size patterns. Lay out the grids on heavy paper or cardboard, and transfer the shape of the piece to the grid, point by point.

Carefully cut the front and bottom, parts number 3 and 4, according to the materials list. Take care to cut all parts to exact size and exactly square (90 degrees). *Stop and recheck all dimensions before going on.* If you have a scroll saw, this will be a very simple project.

Lightly sand all surfaces and edges with medium sandpaper to remove any burrs and all tool marks. Take care to keep *all* edges square and sharp at this time.

After all of the pieces have been carefully made, dry-fit the parts—that is, put the complete project together without glue or nails to check for accuracy and good-fitting joints. If anything needs refitting, now is the time to correct it.

Once all of the parts fit together correctly, assemble the project keeping everything square as you go. Check that all fits are tight.

Finishing

Finish to suit, following the general finishing instructions in the introduction.

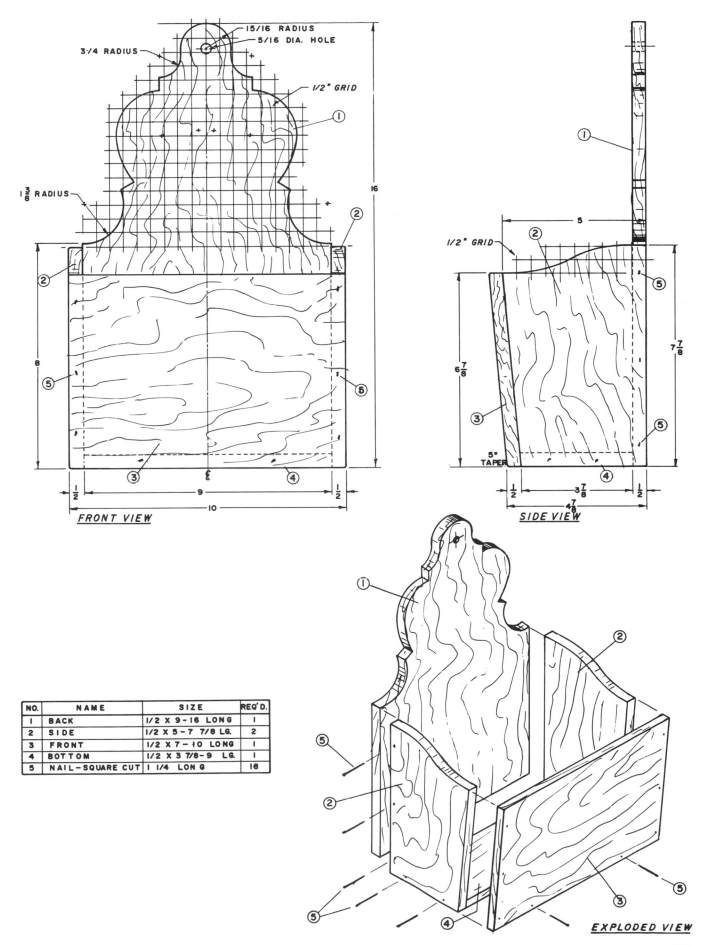

NO.	NAME	SIZE	REQ'D.
1	BACK	1/2 X 9 - 16 LONG	1
2	SIDE	1/2 X 5 - 7 7/8 LG.	2
3	FRONT	1/2 X 7 - 10 LONG	1
4	BOTTOM	1/2 X 3 7/8 - 9 LG.	1
5	NAIL - SQUARE CUT	1 1/4 LONG	18

FRONT VIEW

SIDE VIEW

EXPLODED VIEW

15/16 RADIUS
5/16 DIA. HOLE
3-/4 RADIUS
1/2" GRID
1 3/8 RADIUS
5° TAPER
1/2" GRID

23 ♦ Wall Candle Box with Lid and Leather Hinge

The original of this interesting candle box was made of solid mahogany and had an unusual leather hinge, as shown. I am actually not fond of the leather hinge, but for authenticity I used the leather. I would recommend using two small brass hinges in its place. Gains (notches) need to be cut by mortising into the lid so only the tops of the hinges are seen.

Any hardwood is suitable for this wall box.

Instructions

Study the plans carefully. Note how each part is to be shaped. As you study the plans, try to *visualize* how you will make each part with the tools you have and how the project will be put together.

The back, part number 1, has a lollypop-shape top that will have to be laid out using the given dimensions.

Carefully cut the remaining parts according to the materials list. Take care to cut all parts to exact size and exactly square (90 degrees). *Stop and recheck all dimensions before going on.*

Lightly sand all surfaces and edges with medium sandpaper to remove any burrs and all tool marks. Take care to keep *all* edges square and sharp at this time.

Make all parts following the detailed illustrations and given dimensions. Check all dimensions for accuracy. Resand all over with fine grit sandpaper, still keeping all edges sharp.

After all of the pieces have been carefully made, dry-fit the parts—that is, put the complete project together without glue or nails to check for

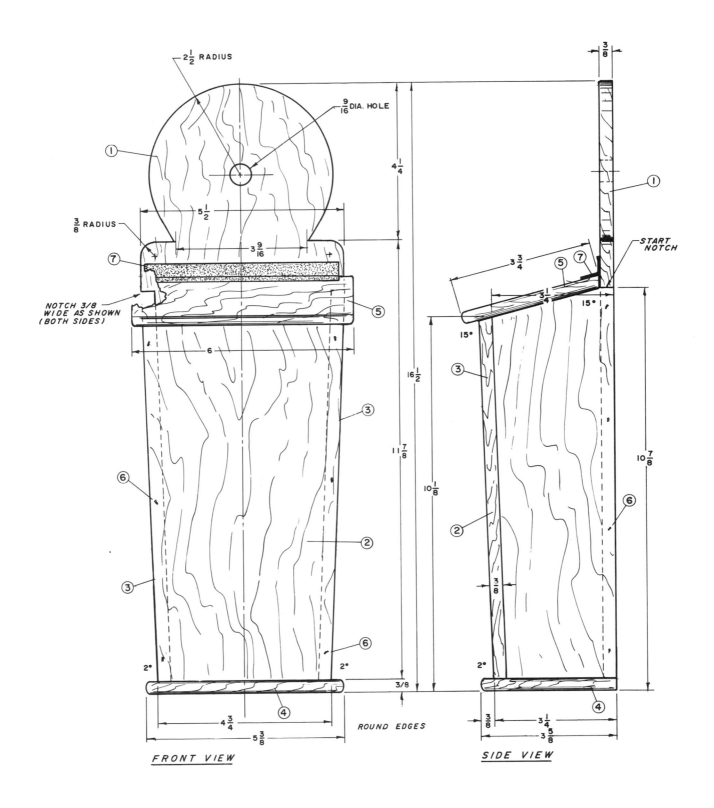

2½ RADIUS

9/16 DIA. HOLE

①

3/8 RADIUS

⑦

NOTCH 3/8
WIDE AS SHOWN
(BOTH SIDES)

5½

3 9/16

4¼

3/8

①

START
NOTCH

3¾

⑤ ⑦

15°

15°

③

3¼

⑤

16½

11⅞

10⅛

6

②

③

⑧

⑥

⑥

②

③

3/8

10⅞

⑥

2°

2°

3/8

3/8

3¼

3⅝

4¾

④

5⅜

ROUND EDGES

④

FRONT VIEW

SIDE VIEW

accuracy and good-fitting joints. If anything needs refitting, now is the time to correct it.

Once all of the parts fit together correctly, assemble the project. Check that all joints are tight.

As noted above, the lid can be attached with a leather hinge, as shown, or with two small brass hinges to suit. If you use the hinges, be sure to cut gains (notches) in the lid, part number 5, to allow for the hinges. If you use leather for the hinges, finish all over *before* adding the leather. I glued *and* tacked the leather in place.

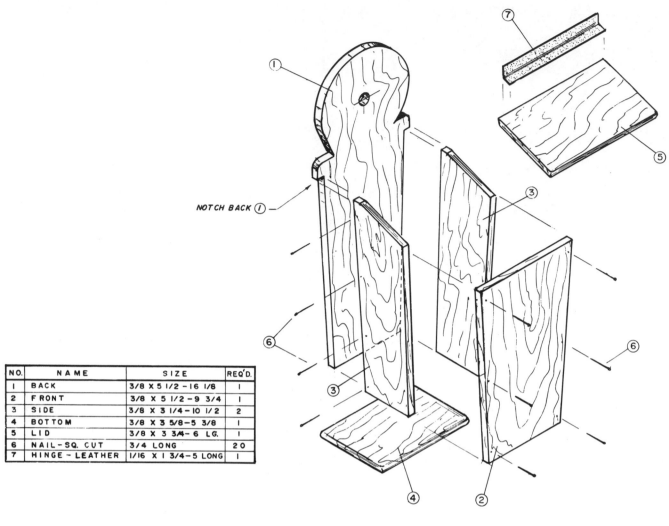

NOTCH BACK ①

NO.	NAME	SIZE	REQ'D.
1	BACK	3/8 X 5 1/2 – 16 1/8	1
2	FRONT	3/8 X 5 1/2 – 9 3/4	1
3	SIDE	3/8 X 3 1/4 – 10 1/2	2
4	BOTTOM	3/8 X 3 5/8 – 5 3/8	1
5	LID	3/8 X 3 3/4 – 6 LG.	1
6	NAIL – SQ. CUT	3/4 LONG	20
7	HINGE – LEATHER	1/16 X 1 3/4 – 5 LONG	1

EXPLODED VIEW

Finishing

Finish to suit, following the general finishing instructions in the introduction. A stained and satin finish is recommended.

WALL PROJECTS WITH DRAWERS AND SHELVES

24 ♦ Double Lollypop-Style Wall Box

This is an example of a *double* lollypop design. It is rather unusual, and yet it is a fine example of the lollypop design. After making my copy, I actually liked the box even more than I thought I would. With its drawer, it is quite a functional wall box.

Instructions

Study the plans carefully. Note how each part is to be shaped and made—especially the drawer parts. As you study the plans, try to *visualize* how you will make each part with the tools you have.

The backboard, part number 1, is the only part that is irregular in shape; it will have to be laid out according to the given dimensions. If you are making only one box, simply lay out the shape directly on the wood.

Carefully cut the remaining parts according to the materials list. Take care to cut all parts to exact size and exactly square (90 degrees). *Stop and recheck all dimensions before going on.*

Lightly sand all surfaces and edges with medium sandpaper to remove any burrs and all tool marks. Take care to keep *all* edges square and sharp at this time.

Shape the parts following the detailed illustrations and given dimensions. Resand all over with fine grit sandpaper, still keeping all edges sharp.

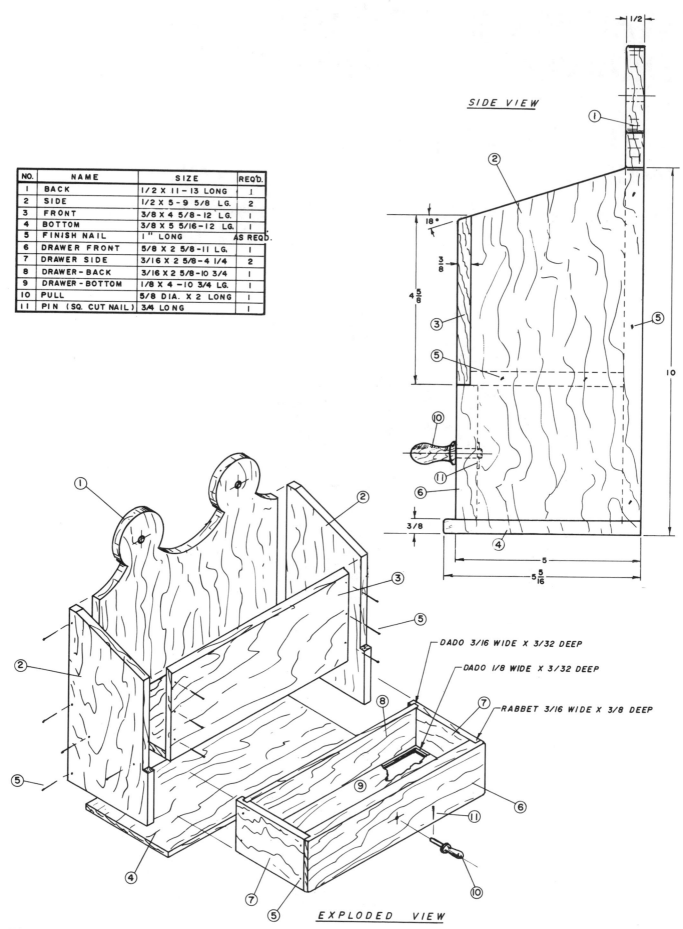

NO.	NAME	SIZE	REQD.
1	BACK	1/2 X 11 - 13 LONG	1
2	SIDE	1/2 X 5 - 9 5/8 LG.	2
3	FRONT	3/8 X 4 5/8 - 12 LG.	1
4	BOTTOM	3/8 X 5 5/16 - 12 LG.	1
5	FINISH NAIL	1" LONG	AS REQD.
6	DRAWER FRONT	5/8 X 2 5/8 - 11 LG.	1
7	DRAWER SIDE	3/16 X 2 5/8 - 4 1/4	2
8	DRAWER - BACK	3/16 X 2 5/8 - 10 3/4	1
9	DRAWER - BOTTOM	1/8 X 4 - 10 3/4 LG.	1
10	PULL	5/8 DIA. X 2 LONG	1
11	PIN (SQ. CUT NAIL)	3/4 LONG	1

SIDE VIEW

18°

3/8

4 5/8

3/8

10

5

5 5/16

DADO 3/16 WIDE X 3/32 DEEP

DADO 1/8 WIDE X 3/32 DEEP

RABBET 3/16 WIDE X 3/8 DEEP

EXPLODED VIEW

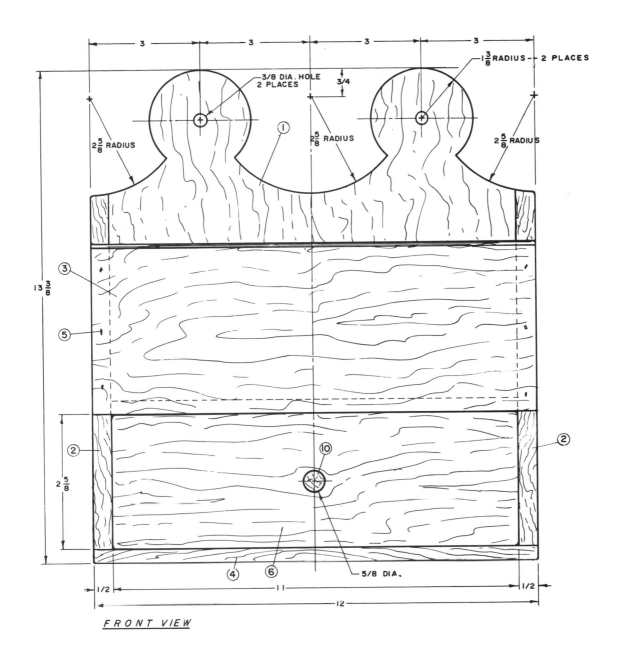

FRONT VIEW

After all of the pieces have been carefully made, dry-fit the parts—that is, put the complete project together without glue or nails to check for accuracy and good-fitting joints. If anything needs refitting, now is the time to correct it.

Once all of the parts fit together correctly, assemble the project keeping everything square as you go. Check that all fits are tight.

Fit the drawer assembly to the box opening—*see* the exploded view.

Finishing

Finish to suit, following the general finishing instructions in the introduction.

25 ◆ Pennsylvania Salt Box, circa 1760

This interesting wall box was originally made by John Dresser of Montgomery County, Pennsylvania, around 1760. The box was pine, painted red with stencil work. The original had snipe hinges, not the pins of this copy. Today it makes a great wall box for keeping all sorts of things and will add a lot to any room.

Instructions

Study the plans carefully. Note how each part is to be shaped. As you study the plans, try to *visualize* how you will make each part with the tools you have.

The back and sides are irregular in shape and will each have to be laid out on a ½-inch grid to make full-size patterns. Lay out the grids on heavy paper or cardboard and transfer the shape of each piece to a grid, point by point.

Carefully cut all of the parts according to the materials list. Take care to cut all parts to exact size and exactly square (90 degrees). *Stop and recheck all dimensions before going on.*

Lightly sand all surfaces and edges with medium sandpaper to remove any burrs and all tool marks. Take care to keep *all* edges square and sharp at this time.

Make the parts following the detailed illustrations and given dimensions. Once the full-size patterns for the back and sides have been transferred to the wood, cut out those pieces. Check all dimensions for accuracy. Resand all over with fine grit sandpaper, still keeping all edges sharp.

After all of the pieces have been carefully made, dry-fit the parts—that is, put the complete project together without glue or nails to check for accuracy and good-fitting joints. If anything needs refitting, now is the time to correct it.

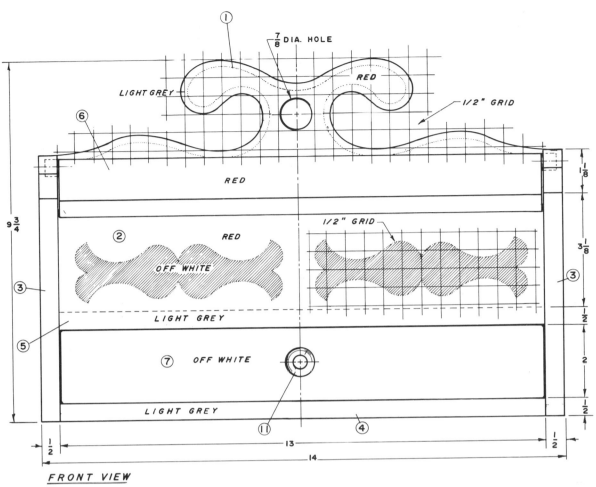

① ⑦/₈ DIA. HOLE

LIGHT GREY   RED

1/2" GRID

⑥   RED

② RED   1/2" GRID

OFF WHITE

9³⁄₄   ③   ③

⑤   1 ¹⁄₈

3 ¹⁄₈

1⁄₂

⑦ OFF WHITE   2

LIGHT GREY   1⁄₂

⑪   ④

1⁄₂   13   1⁄₂

14

FRONT VIEW

NO.	NAME	SIZE	REQ'D.
1	BACK	1/2 X 9 3/4-13 LONG	1
2	FRONT	1/2 X 3 1/8-13 LONG	1
3	SIDE	1/2 X 5-7 1/4 LONG	2
4	BOTTOM	1/2 X 4 1/2-13 LONG	1
5	DIVIDER	1/2 X 4-13 LONG	1
6	LID	1/2 X 4 3/4-13 1/2	1
7	DRAWER FRONT	1/2 X 2-13 LONG	1
8	DRAWER SIDE	3/8 X 2-4 1/4 LG.	2
9	DRAWER BACK	3/8 X 2-12 3/4 LG.	1
10	DRAWER BOTTOM	1/4 X 4-12 3/4 LG.	1
11	PULL W/ PIN	3/4 X 1 1/4 LONG	1
12	FINISH NAIL	1" LONG (SQ.CUT) AS REQ'D	

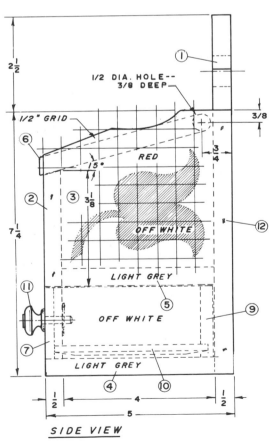

①

2 ¹⁄₂

1/2 DIA. HOLE--
3/8 DEEP

1/2" GRID   3/8

⑥   RED   3⁄₄

15°   ③ 3 ¹⁄₈

② OFF WHITE   ⑫

7 ¹⁄₄   LIGHT GREY

⑤

⑪   OFF WHITE   ⑨

⑦   LIGHT GREY

④   ⑩

1⁄₂   4   1⁄₂

5

SIDE VIEW

81

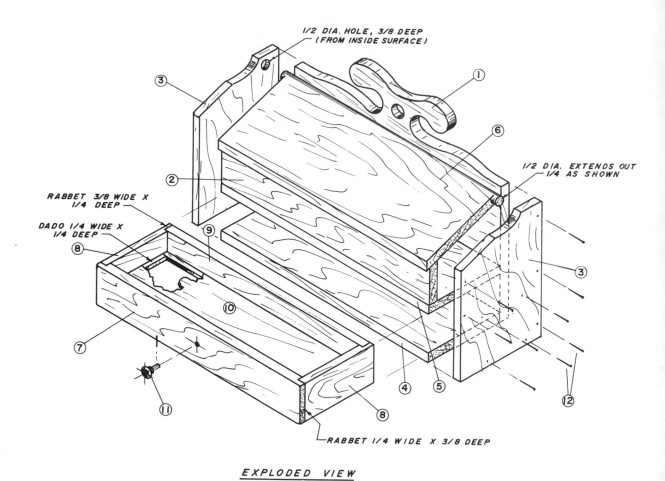

1/2 DIA. HOLE, 3/8 DEEP
(FROM INSIDE SURFACE)

1/2 DIA. EXTENDS OUT
1/4 AS SHOWN

RABBET 3/8 WIDE X
1/4 DEEP

DADO 1/4 WIDE X
1/4 DEEP

RABBET 1/4 WIDE X 3/8 DEEP

EXPLODED VIEW

Once all of the parts fit together correctly, assemble the project starting with the two sides and lid, keeping everything square as you go. Check that all fits are tight.

Finishing

Prime the box, and apply a top coat of off-white paint. Paint the red area, as indicated, and, after it dries, add the gray trim, as shown.

Carefully lay out the two stencil patterns on ½-inch grids, and cut them out. Stencil them on the box, as shown. When everything is dry, lightly sand the edges of the box to simulate "wear." Apply a light coat of walnut stain over the entire box to add a "250-year-old" look. If you have never done any stencilling, there are many good books that you can buy or borrow from your local library for details on how to stencil.

26♦Vermont Wall Box with Drawer

The original of this wall box is made of knotty pine. I'm not so sure that the original is all that old, but with its curved drawer front, I thought it offered an interestingly different variation on the wall box theme. My copy is made of walnut with a maple drawer front to accent the curved front. As with many wall boxes, this one is very easy to make.

Instructions

Study the plans carefully. Note how each part is to be shaped. As you study the plans, try to *visualize* how you will make each part with the tools you have.

The back and sides, parts number 1 and 2, are irregular in shape and will have to be laid out on ½-inch grids to make full-size patterns. Lay out the grids on heavy paper or cardboard and transfer the shape of each piece to a grid, point by point.

Carefully cut all of the parts according to the materials list. Take care to cut all parts to exact size and exactly square (90 degrees). *Stop and recheck all dimensions before going on.*

Lightly sand all surfaces and edges with medium sandpaper to remove all tool marks. Take care to keep *all* edges square and sharp at this time.

On this project, because of the curved drawer front, I worked "backwards"—that is, I made the *drawer assembly first* and fitted the case around the drawer front. Lay out the bottom, part number 3, from the drawer front—about ¼ inch away from the drawer front. *See* the view at A–A.

Make the parts following the given dimensions. Transfer the full-size patterns to the wood, and cut out the pieces. Check all dimensions for accuracy. Resand all over with fine grit sandpaper, still keeping all edges sharp.

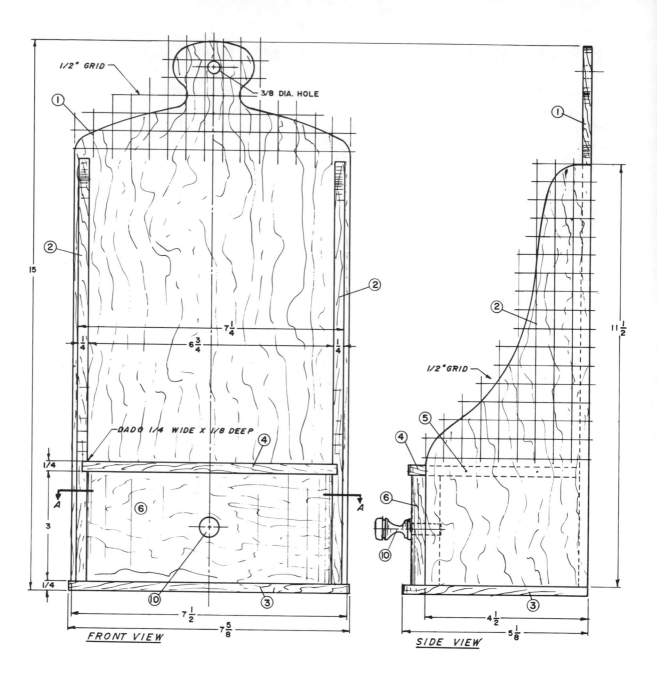

1/2" GRID

3/8 DIA. HOLE

15

7 1/4

6 3/4

1/4   1/4

DADO 1/4 WIDE X 1/8 DEEP

1/4

A

3

1/4

7 1/2

7 5/8

FRONT VIEW

1/2" GRID

11 1/2

SIDE VIEW

4 1/2

5 1/8

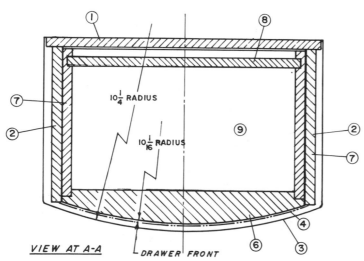

10 1/4 RADIUS

10 1/16 RADIUS

VIEW AT A-A

DRAWER FRONT

NO.	NAME	SIZE	REQ'D.
1	BACK	1/4 X 7 1/2-14 3/4	1
2	SIDE	1/4 X 4 1/2-11 1/2 LG.	2
3	BOTTOM	1/4 X 5 1/8-7 5/8 LG.	1
4	SHELF	1/4 X 4 3/4-7 LONG	1
5	BRAD	3/4 LONG	AS REQ'D.
6	DRAWER FRONT	3/4 X 3-6 3/4 LONG	1
7	DRAWER SIDE	1/4 X 3-4 LONG	2
8	DRAWER BACK	1/4 X 3-6 1/2 LONG	1
9	DRAWER BOTTOM	1/8 X 3 3/4-6 1/2 LG	1
10	PULL	1/2 DIA. X 1 3/4 LG.	1

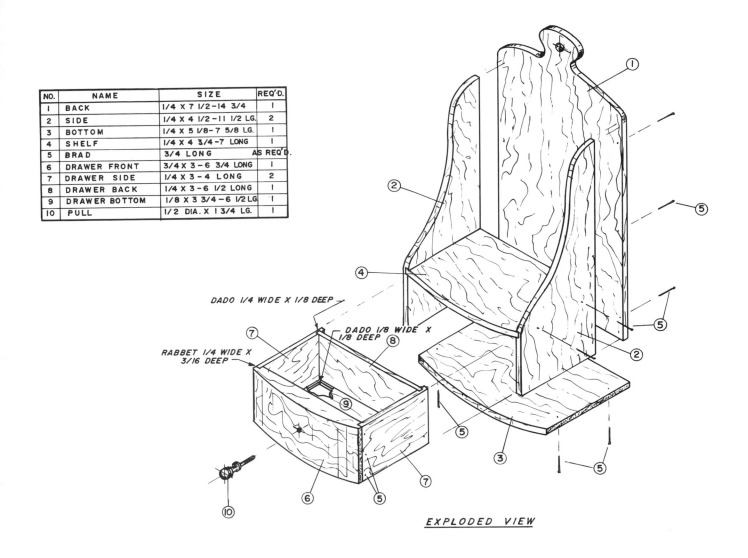

DADO 1/4 WIDE X 1/8 DEEP

DADO 1/8 WIDE X 1/8 DEEP

RABBET 1/4 WIDE X 3/16 DEEP

EXPLODED VIEW

After all of the pieces have been carefully made, dry-fit the parts—that is, put the complete project together without glue or nails to check for accuracy and good-fitting joints. If anything needs refitting, now is the time to correct it. Be sure the drawer assembly fits correctly.

The drawer pull, part number 10, can either be purchased or turned on a lathe.

Once all of the parts fit together correctly, assemble the project, keeping everything square as you go. Check that all fits are tight.

Finishing

Finish to suit, following the general finishing instructions in the introduction.

27 ◆ Salt Box with Lid, circa 1800

This is not just another salt box. It is a very different and interesting wall box that has a Queen Anne influence. I found it in New England and estimate that it was made around 1800 or so, judging by the somewhat "formal" design and because it is made of solid walnut. The hinges are mounted on top in my copy just as in the original—I would prefer mortising gains (notches) for the hinges so that they are set flush, but my interest was in reproducing the original. If you do not care to copy the original exactly, then I suggest you set the hinges flush. This box makes a great formal wall box for all sorts of things, adding a lot to any room.

Instructions

Study the plans carefully. Note how each part is to be shaped. As you study the plans, try to *visualize* how you will make each part.

The back and sides are irregular in shape and will have to be laid out on 1-inch grids to make full-size patterns. Lay out the grids on heavy paper or cardboard, and transfer the shape of each piece to a grid, point by point.

Carefully cut all parts according to the materials list. Take care to cut all parts to exact size and exactly square (90 degrees). *Stop and recheck all dimensions before going on.*

Lightly sand all surfaces and edges with medium sandpaper to remove any burrs and all tool marks. Take care to keep *all* edges square and sharp at this time.

Make the parts following the detailed illustrations and given dimensions. Transfer full-size patterns of the back and sides to the wood, and cut out the pieces. Check all dimensions for accuracy. Resand all over with fine grit sandpaper, still keeping all edges sharp.

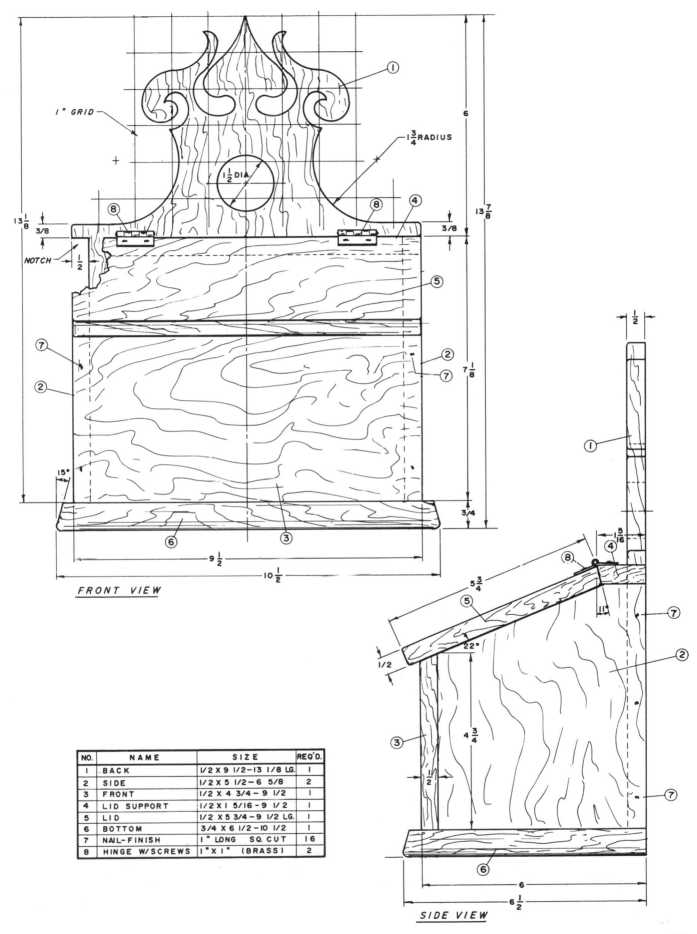

NO.	NAME	SIZE	REQ'D.
1	BACK	1/2 X 9 1/2 - 13 1/8 LG.	1
2	SIDE	1/2 X 5 1/2 - 6 5/8	2
3	FRONT	1/2 X 4 3/4 - 9 1/2	1
4	LID SUPPORT	1/2 X 1 5/16 - 9 1/2	1
5	LID	1/2 X 5 3/4 - 9 1/2 LG.	1
6	BOTTOM	3/4 X 6 1/2 - 10 1/2	1
7	NAIL-FINISH	1" LONG SQ. CUT	16
8	HINGE W/SCREWS	1"X 1" (BRASS)	2

FRONT VIEW

SIDE VIEW

1" GRID

1 3/4 RADIUS

1 1/2 DIA

NOTCH

87

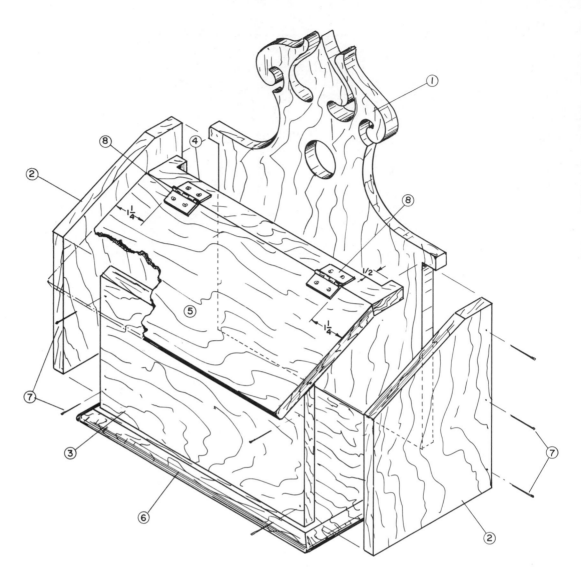

EXPLODED VIEW

After all of the pieces have been carefully made, dry-fit the parts—that is, put the complete project together without glue or nails to check for accuracy and good-fitting joints. If anything needs refitting, now is the time to correct it.

Once all of the parts fit together correctly, assemble the project starting with the back, part number 1. Then attach the two sides, parts number 2, followed by the front, part number 3, and the bottom, part number 6.

Attach the lid, part number 5, to the lid support, part number 4, with the two hinges, parts number 8. Add the lid and lid support, parts number 5, 6, and 8, to the box assembly.

Check that the lid works correctly.

Finishing

Remove the lid and hinges. Lightly sand all over. If you used a hardwood such as walnut, cherry, or maple, I suggest applying a clear satin top coat. Add the lid and hinges and a coat of paste wax.

28 ◆ Pennsylvania Pipe Box

Antique pipe boxes are becoming rare. When they do come up for sale, they are often quite expensive—so much so that they are increasingly found in museums only. These early pipe boxes, like early wall boxes, come in all shapes and sizes. They are made of just about all kinds of wood, typically hardwood. They were used to store the long clay pipes of Colonial days. Most had a drawer below to store the tobacco. Today pipe boxes make a perfect place to store candles and matches in the event of a power failure. Friends of mine uses theirs for outgoing mail with stamps stored in the drawer.

Instructions

Study the plans carefully. Note how each part is to be shaped. As you study the plans, try to *visualize* how you will make each part.

The parts that are irregular in shape—the back, sides, and front, parts number 1, 2, and 3—should each be laid out on a ½-inch grid to make a full-size pattern. Lay out the grids on heavy paper or cardboard, and transfer the shape of each piece to a grid, point by point.

Carefully cut the parts according to the materials list. Take care to cut all parts to exact size and exactly square (90 degrees). *Stop and recheck all dimensions before going on.*

Lightly sand all surfaces and edges with medium sandpaper to remove any burrs and all tool marks. Take care to keep *all* edges square and sharp at this time.

Make the parts following the detailed illustrations and given dimensions. Transfer the full-size patterns to the wood, and cut out the pieces. Check all dimensions for accuracy. Resand all over with fine grit sandpaper, still keeping all edges sharp.

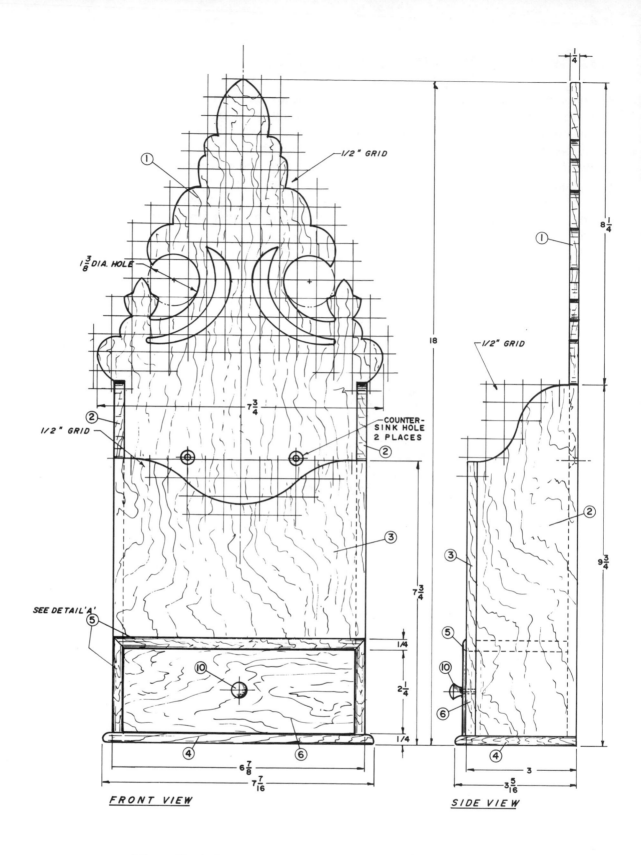

FRONT VIEW

SIDE VIEW

After all of the pieces have been carefully made, dry-fit the parts—that is, put the complete project together without glue or nails to check for accuracy and good-fitting joints. If anything needs refitting, now is the time to correct it.

Once all of the parts fit together correctly, assemble the project, keeping everything square as you go. Check that all fits are tight.

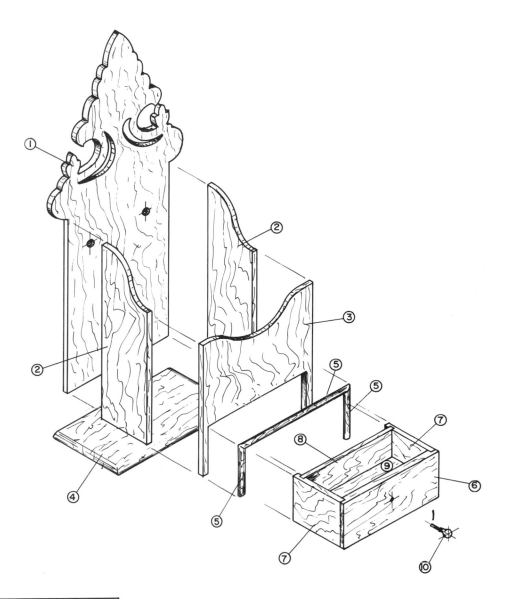

NO.	NAME	SIZE	REQ'D.
1	BACK	1/4 X 7 3/4 – 17 3/4 LG.	1
2	SIDE	1/4 X 2 3/4 – 9 1/2 LG	2
3	FRONT	1/4 X 6 7/8 – 7 1/2 LG.	1
4	BASE	1/4 X 3 5/16 – 7 7/16	1
5	MOLDING	1/8 X 1/4 – 16 LONG	1
6	DRAWER FRONT	3/8 X 2 1/4 – 6 3/8 LG.	1
7	DRAWER – SIDE	3/16 X 2 1/4 – 2 5/8	2
8	DRAWER–BACK	3/16 X 2 1/4 – 6 1/8	1
9	DRAWER–BOTTOM	1/8 X 2 1/8 – 6 1/8 LG.	1
10	PULL W/ PIN	7/16 DIA. X 1" LONG	1

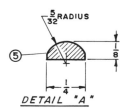

DETAIL "A"

Add the moulding, part number 5, around the drawer opening, as shown. Fit the drawer assembly to the case.

Finishing

Finish to suit, following the general finishing instructions in the introduction.

29 ♦ Spoon Rack with Drawer

In days past, simple folk did not use forks or knives—they only had spoons. In early America, there were very few places to store utensils; so the spoon rack came into its own as the place to keep spoons in racks on the wall between meals. This copy of an original spoon rack holds twelve spoons. Today it makes a great place to display a collection of antique or ornamental spoons. This project can be stained and finished if you use a suitable hardwood—the original was made of walnut but painted, however. This project would look great with a worn "crackle"-painted finish.

Instructions

Study the plans carefully. Note how each part is to be shaped. As you study the plans, try to *visualize* how you will make each part with the tools you have, and how the project is to be assembled. Note which parts you will put together first, second, and so on, and how the drawer is made.

Parts that are irregular in shape or that have cutouts should be laid out on 1-inch grids to make full-size patterns. Lay out the grids on heavy paper, or draw directly on the wood.

Carefully cut all of the parts according to the materials list. Take care to cut all parts to exact size and exactly square (90 degrees). *Stop and recheck all dimensions before going on.*

Lightly sand all surfaces and edges with medium sandpaper to remove any burrs and all tool marks. Take care to keep *all* edges square and sharp at this time.

Make the parts following the detailed illustrations and given dimensions. Take care to make a *matched pair* of sides—that is, one right-hand and one left-hand side. Make *stop* dadoes and rabbets in the interior surfaces of the sides, as shown in the drawings.

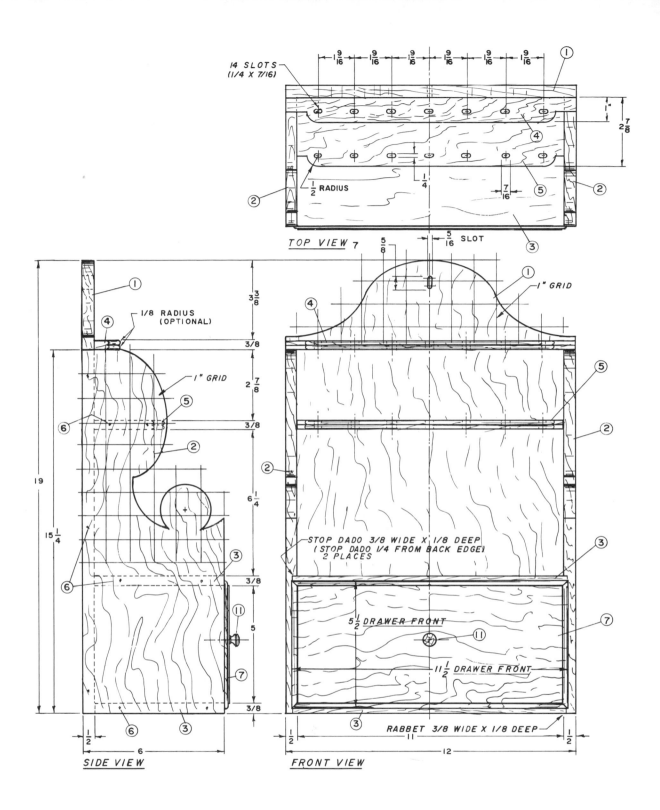

TOP VIEW

SIDE VIEW

FRONT VIEW

14 SLOTS
(1/4 X 7/16)

$\frac{9}{16}$ $\frac{9}{16}$ $\frac{9}{16}$ $\frac{9}{16}$ $\frac{9}{16}$ $\frac{9}{16}$

$1''$

$2\frac{7}{8}$

$\frac{1}{2}$ RADIUS

$\frac{1}{4}$

$\frac{7}{16}$

$\frac{5}{16}$ SLOT

$\frac{5}{8}$

1" GRID

1/8 RADIUS
(OPTIONAL)

1" GRID

$3\frac{3}{8}$

$2\frac{7}{8}$

$\frac{3}{8}$

$\frac{3}{8}$

$6\frac{1}{4}$

$\frac{3}{8}$

5

$\frac{3}{8}$

19

$15\frac{1}{4}$

$\frac{1}{2}$

6

STOP DADO 3/8 WIDE X 1/8 DEEP
(STOP DADO 1/4 FROM BACK EDGE)
2 PLACES

$5\frac{1}{2}$ DRAWER FRONT

$11\frac{1}{2}$ DRAWER FRONT

RABBET 3/8 WIDE X 1/8 DEEP

$\frac{1}{2}$ 11 $\frac{1}{2}$

12

NO.	NAME	SIZE	REQ'D.
1	BACK	1/2 X 12 - 19 LONG	1
2	SIDE	1/2 X 6 -15 1/4 LG.	2
3	SHELF / BOTTOM	3/8 X 5 1/2 - 11 LG.	2
4	TOP SHELF	3/8 X 1 - 11 LONG	1
5	MIDDLE SHELF	3/8 X 2 7/8 - 11 LG	1
6	FINISH NAIL	6d	18
7	DRAWER FRONT	5/8 X 5 1/2 - 11 1/2 LG.	1
8	DRAWER SIDE	1/4 X 5 - 5 3/8 LG.	2
9	DRAWER BACK	1/4 X 5 - 10 3/4 LG.	1
10	DRAWER BOTTOM	1/4 X 5 3/16 - 10 3/4	1
11	PULL	3/8 DIA. X 7/8 LG.	1

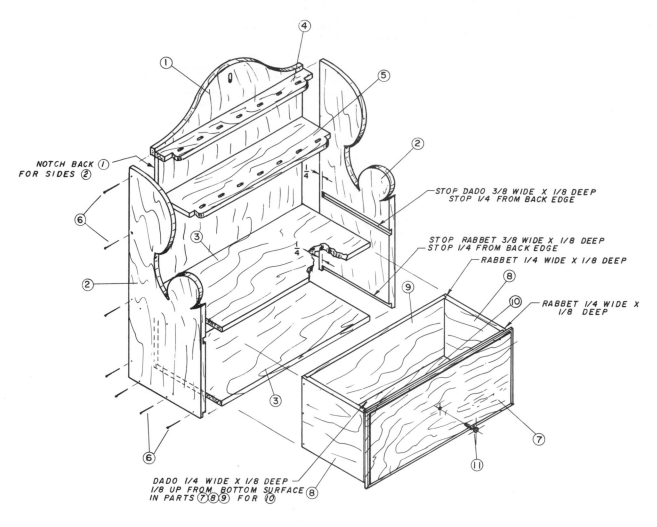

NOTCH BACK
FOR SIDES ②

STOP DADO 3/8 WIDE X 1/8 DEEP
STOP 1/4 FROM BACK EDGE

STOP RABBET 3/8 WIDE X 1/8 DEEP
STOP 1/4 FROM BACK EDGE

RABBET 1/4 WIDE X 1/8 DEEP

RABBET 1/4 WIDE X
1/8 DEEP

DADO 1/4 WIDE X 1/8 DEEP
1/8 UP FROM BOTTOM SURFACE
IN PARTS ⑦⑧⑨ FOR ⑩

EXPLODED VIEW

Locate and cut the seven ¼-inch by ⁷⁄₁₆-inch slots in the shelves—parts number 4 and 5.

Assemble the project keeping everything square as you go. Check that the shelves and sides are square to the backboard—parts number 1, 2, 3, 4, and 5.

Make the drawer assembly using the actual drawer opening to determine the finished size. The given dimensions are approximate and the size of your drawer opening may be slightly different.

The drawer pull, part number 11, can be either purchased or made. Anything approximately ⅜ inch in diameter is suitable.

Finishing

Finish to suit, following the general finishing instructions in the introduction.

30 ◆ Early Fretwork Wall Shelf

Fretwork projects such as this and the one following were very popular around 1880 or so. They became popular again in the 1930s. Very early patterns were cut with a foot-powered scroll saw—later, in the thirties and forties, the electric jigsaw was used to cut them out. This example is a simple fretwork wall shelf.

Instructions

Study the plans carefully. Note how each part is to be shaped.

The back piece, part number 1, is irregular in shape and should be laid out on a 1-inch grid to make a full-size pattern. Lay out the grid on heavy paper or cardboard, and transfer the shape of the piece to the grid, point by point.

Carefully cut all parts to overall size according to the materials list. Lightly sand all surfaces and edges with medium sandpaper to remove all tool marks.

I have had good luck by finishing the surfaces at this time, *before* cutting the pieces out. I add a coat of wood filler, sand all over, and apply a top coat or two of satin finish. I then resand, and apply the pattern. It is easier to get a pleasing finish on the outer surface at this time rather than after cutting out the pattern. A final light sanding and top coat will have to be added after cutting out.

Transfer the full-size patterns to the wood, and cut out the pieces. For fretwork projects such as these, I usually make a full-size copy of the design on paper, glue it directly on the wood, and cut it out. I then remove the paper and sand all over.

Lay out and cut out the shelf following the detailed drawings and given dimensions.

Fit the pieces together and assemble the shelves, keeping everything square. Check that all fits are tight.

If you use a hardwood, be sure to drill small holes for the finishing nails or brads, so that the wood will not split.

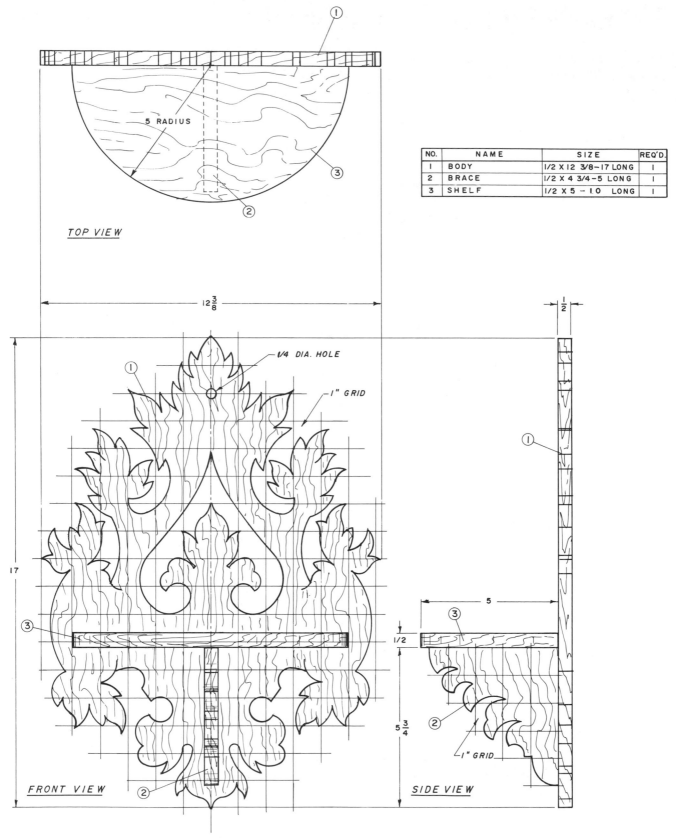

TOP VIEW

5 RADIUS

NO.	NAME	SIZE	REQ'D.
1	BODY	1/2 X 12 3/8 – 17 LONG	1
2	BRACE	1/2 X 4 3/4 – 5 LONG	1
3	SHELF	1/2 X 5 – 1.0 LONG	1

12 3/8

1/4 DIA. HOLE

1" GRID

17

5

1/2

5 3/4

1" GRID

FRONT VIEW

SIDE VIEW

Finishing

Finish to suit, following the general finishing instructions in the introduction. If you finished the surfaces *before* cutting out, simply sand lightly all over, and apply a light top coat of satin finish.

31◆Early Fretwork Corner Wall Shelf

Fretwork projects such as this and the one preceding were very popular around 1880 or so. They became popular again in the 1930s. Very early patterns were cut with a foot-powered scroll saw—later, in the thirties and forties, the electric jigsaw was used to cut them out. This example is a fretwork corner wall shelf.

Instructions

The back piece, part number 1, is irregular in shape and should be laid out on a ½-inch grid to make a full-size pattern. Lay out the grid on heavy paper or cardboard, and transfer the shape of the piece to the grid, point by point.

Carefully cut all parts to overall size according to the materials list. Lightly sand all surfaces and edges with medium sandpaper to remove all tool marks.

I have had good luck by finishing the surfaces at this time, *before* cutting the pieces out. I add a coat of wood filler, sand all over, and apply a top coat or two of satin finish. I then resand, and apply the pattern. It is easier to get a pleasing finish on the outer surface at this time rather than after cutting out the pattern. A final light sanding and top coat will have to be added after cutting out.

Transfer the full-size patterns to the wood, and cut out the pieces. For fretwork projects such as these, I usually make a full-size copy of the design on paper, glue it directly on the wood, and cut it out. I then remove the paper and sand all over.

Tack the two sides together with small brads before cutting out, so you will get two sides *exactly* the same size and shape.

Lay out and cut out the shelves following the detailed drawings and given dimensions.

Fit the pieces together and assemble the shelves, keeping everything square. Check that all fits are tight.

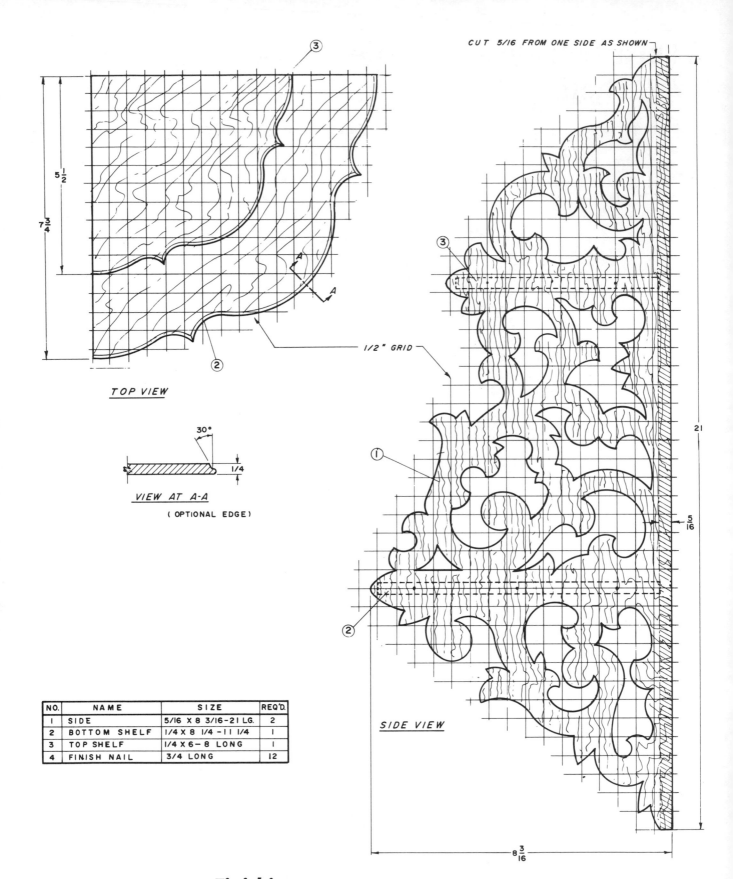

NO.	NAME	SIZE	REQ'D.
1	SIDE	5/16 X 8 3/16 – 21 LG.	2
2	BOTTOM SHELF	1/4 X 8 1/4 – 11 1/4	1
3	TOP SHELF	1/4 X 6 – 8 LONG	1
4	FINISH NAIL	3/4 LONG	12

Finishing

Finish to suit, following the general finishing instructions in the introduction. If you finished the surfaces *before* cutting out, simply sand lightly all over, and apply a light top coat of satin finish.

32 ♦ Canted Wall Box with Shelves

As noted before, I am always looking for projects that are different. I really like this box, even though I'm not sure *where* to use it. I found it years ago, and I cannot even remember where I found it. According to my notes, the original was very large, so I had to scale it down. The original was 34½ inches high—this one is a two-thirds version (66.6 percent of original size). It was made around 1840 and was painted.

Instructions

Cut to overall size the sides, parts number 2, and lay out the two inside dadoes and one rabbet on each. Note that the dadoes and rabbets are *blind*—that is, they are *not* cut to the back edge. *See* the exploded view.

Make the two dado and one rabbet cut on the *inside* surfaces of the two sides. Be sure to make one right-hand and one left-hand side. Make these cuts before cutting the outside shape of the sides so that you will have a straight edge to line up against your fence.

The back and sides, parts number 1 and 2, are irregular in shape and will have to be laid out on a ½-inch grid to make full-size patterns. Lay out the grids on heavy paper or cardboard, and transfer the shape of each piece to the grid, point by point.

Transfer the full-size patterns to the wood, and carefully cut out the pieces. Sand all over with fine grit sandpaper, keeping all edges sharp.

Don't forget to cut the two notches along the sides of the back, part number 1, for the sides, parts number 2, to fit into.

Carefully line up the dado and rabbet cuts, and tape the two sides together with the cuts on the inside. Draw the pattern on the outside surface, and cut out both sides at the same time. Sand the edges while they are still taped together.

Cut the three shelves to size according to the materials list. Take care to cut all parts to exact size and exactly square (90 degrees). *Stop and recheck*

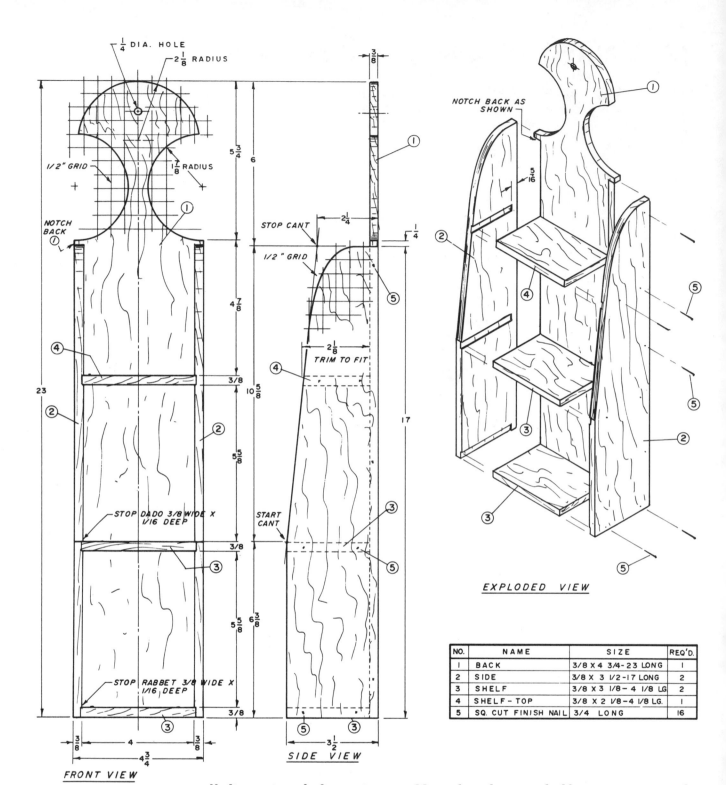

NO.	NAME	SIZE	REQ'D.
1	BACK	3/8 X 4 3/4 - 23 LONG	1
2	SIDE	3/8 X 3 1/2 - 17 LONG	2
3	SHELF	3/8 X 3 1/8 - 4 1/8 LG.	2
4	SHELF - TOP	3/8 X 2 1/8 - 4 1/8 LG.	1
5	SQ. CUT FINISH NAIL	3/4 LONG	16

all dimensions before going on. Note that the top shelf is cut at an angle along its front edge to match the sides.

Lightly sand all surfaces and edges with medium sandpaper to remove all tool marks. Take care to keep *all* edges square and sharp.

After all of the pieces have been carefully made, dry-fit the parts—that is, put the complete project together without glue or nails to check for accuracy and good-fitting joints. If anything needs refitting, now is the time to correct it.

Once all of the parts fit together correctly, assemble the project, keeping everything square as you go. Check that all fits are tight.

100

33 ◆ Wall Shelf with Drawers

I first saw this wall shelf years ago, before I started writing woodworking books. It was in the Shelburne Museum in Vermont. I really liked it and took a few notes and made a photograph of it. For years, I wanted to make a copy, but I didn't have enough information to correctly build it. I wanted a wall shelf for this book so while I was researching wall shelves that I had photographed and measured in the past, I came across the old photograph of this one. My interest in it was rekindled, and fueled by my desire to use it here, I went back to the Shelburne Museum to find and measure it. Luckily, it was still there; so here it is!

I painted the interior of my copy a light soldier blue and the outside a brick red color. To make it look old and worn, I distressed it and sanded the edges slightly.

Instructions

Study the plans carefully. Note how each part is to be shaped. As you study the plans, try to *visualize* how you will make each part, and how the project will be assembled. Note which parts you will put together first, second, and so on—exactly how *you* will put it together. Except for the drawers, it is rather easy to make. Note that you can use two, three, or four boards—parts number 9—for the back according to the widths you have available or as desired.

The sides, parts number 1, are irregular in shape and will have to be laid out on a 1-inch grid to make a full-size pattern—only one pattern is needed. Lay out the grid on heavy paper or cardboard, and transfer the shape of the piece to the grid, point by point.

Cut the two side boards to the given overall size according to the materials list, and carefully locate and make the three dado cuts and two rabbet cuts following the given dimensions. Cut the rabbet along the back edge as shown at this time. *Important: Be sure to make one right-hand and one left-hand side.*

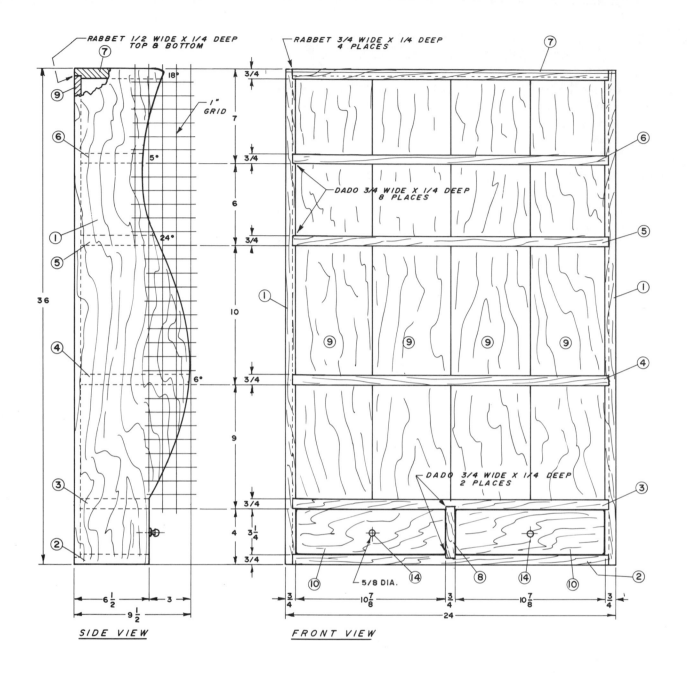

SIDE VIEW

FRONT VIEW

After the dadoes and rabbets have been cut, tack the two side pieces together—be sure to line up the dado cuts. Transfer the pattern to the wood, and carefully cut out the two sides at the same time. Sand the edges while the sides are still attached to each other. Check all dimensions for accuracy. Resand all over with fine grit sandpaper, keeping all edges sharp.

Carefully cut the remaining parts to size according to the materials list. Take care to cut all parts to exact size and exactly square (90 degrees). *Stop and recheck all dimensions before going on.*

If you would like plate grooves in your shelves, now is the time to cut them into the top surface of the shelves. Although not present in the original, a groove ½ inch wide and ¼ inch deep, out 1½ inches from the back edge, would make a suitable plate groove for each shelf.

Lightly sand all surfaces and edges with medium sandpaper to remove all tool marks. Take care to keep *all* edges square and sharp.

NO.	NAME	SIZE	REQ'D
1	SIDE	3/4 X 9 1/2 - 36 LG.	2
2	SHELF	3/4 X 6 1/2 - 23 LG.	1
3	SHELF	3/4 X 6 - 23 LONG	1
4	SHELF	3/4 X 9 - 23 LONG	1
5	SHELF	3/4 X 6 7/8 - 23 LG.	1
6	SHELF	3/4 X 5 5/8 - 23 LG.	1
7	TOP	3/4 X 7 1/2 - 23 LG.	1
8	DIVIDER	3/4 X 6 - 3 3/4 LG.	1
9	BACK	1/2 X 5 3/4 - 35 LG.	4
10	DRAWER FRONT	1/2 X 3 1/4 - 10 7/8 LG.	2
11	DRAWER SIDE	3/8 X 3 1/4 - 5 1/4	4
12	DRAWER BACK	3/8 X 3 1/4 - 10 1/2	2
13	DRAWER BOTTOM	1/4 X 5 - 10 1/2 LG	2
14	PULL	5/8 DIA. X 1 9/16	2
15	PIN	TO SUIT	2

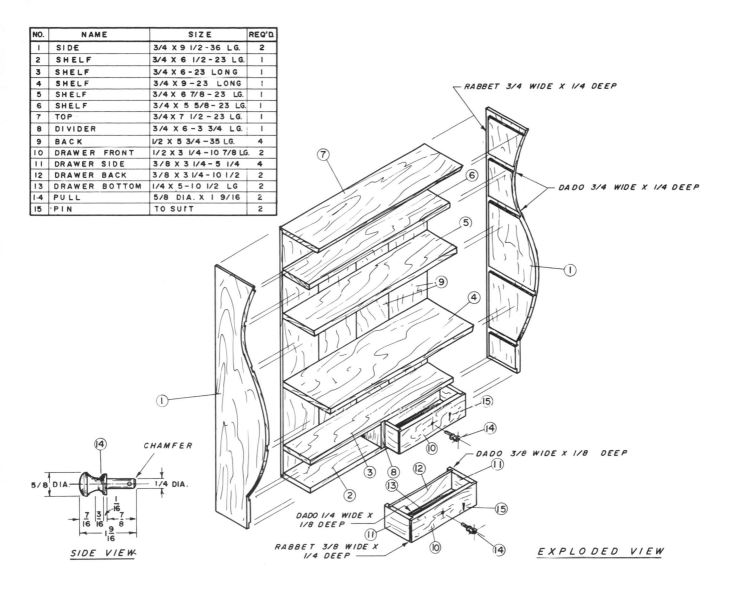

After all of the pieces have been carefully made, dry-fit the parts—that is, put the complete project together without glue or nails to check for accuracy and good-fitting joints. If anything needs refitting, now is the time to correct it.

Once all of the parts fit together correctly, assemble the project, keeping everything square as you go. Check that all fits are tight.

Fit the drawers to the openings. Use the given dimensions as a guide as your drawer openings may vary slightly. The original drawers had dovetail joints—this one uses simple rabbet joints.

The drawer pulls, parts number 14, can be either purchased or turned on a lathe according to the given dimensions for the pull.

Finishing

Finish to suit, following the general finishing instructions in the introduction. The original was painted two-tone—noted above are the colors I used on my copy. If you used a fine hardwood and hate to paint over it, I suggest staining the outside. This will accent the wood and grain pattern. But I would still paint the interior walls.

WALL MIRROR PROJECTS

34 ◆ Gothic Wall Mirror

In my search for unusual and different projects to make, I was delighted to find this Gothic wall mirror. Now this one *is* different. My wife *hates* it, but I like it—in the right setting it can be *great!* It is simple to make since it is cut out of one piece of wood.

Instructions

Study the plans carefully. Note how the body is irregularly shaped. It will have to be laid out on a ½-inch grid to make a full-size pattern. Lay out the grid on heavy paper or cardboard, and transfer the shape of the piece to the grid, point by point.

Transfer the full-size pattern to the wood, and carefully cut out the body. Check all dimensions for accuracy. Sand all over with fine grit sandpaper, keeping all edges sharp.

Carefully cut the interior for the mirror. Sand all edges smooth.

Using a router and a 45-degree cutter with a ball-bearing follower, cut the 45-degree bevel all around the body, inside and outside.

Using the router and a ⁵⁄₁₆-inch rabbet cutter with a ball-bearing follower, cut a rabbet ⁵⁄₁₆ inch wide and ⁵⁄₁₆ inch deep as shown. You will have to chisel out square corners to get a clean rectangular notch and flat surface in the back for the mirror and backing, parts number 2 and 3.

Cut out a backboard, part number 3, to fit the opening. Make a 10-degree bevel cut on the outside surface along all four edges of the backboard, as the original had.

Cut a piece of mirror to *loosely* fit into the opening—be sure it is *not* a tight fit, since the mirror might break if the wood expands or contracts.

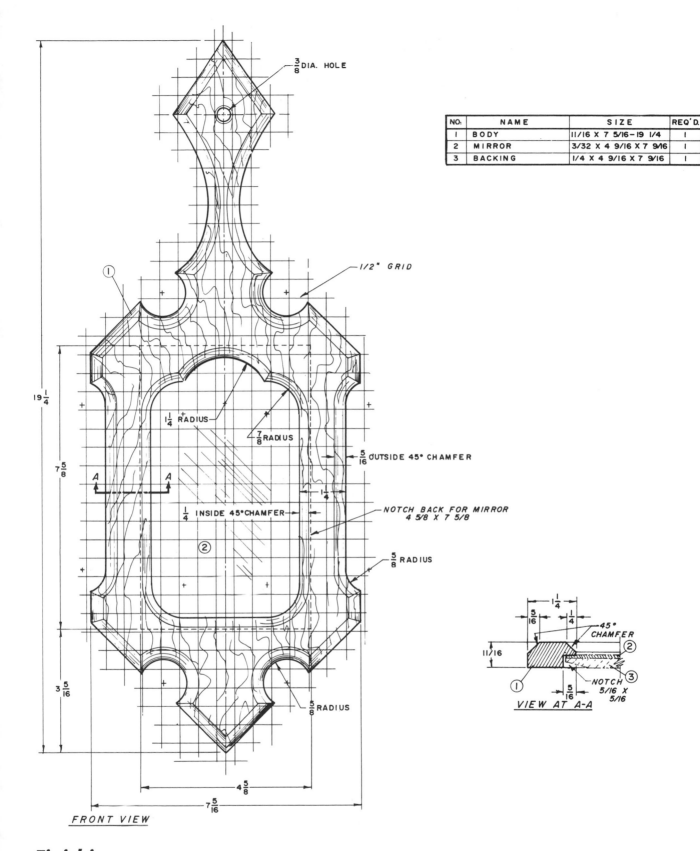

NO.	NAME	SIZE	REQ'D.
1	BODY	11/16 X 7 5/16 – 19 1/4	1
2	MIRROR	3/32 X 4 9/16 X 7 9/16	1
3	BACKING	1/4 X 4 9/16 X 7 9/16	1

3/8 DIA. HOLE

1/2" GRID

1/4 RADIUS

7/8 RADIUS

5/16 OUTSIDE 45° CHAMFER

A   A

1/4 INSIDE 45° CHAMFER

1/4

NOTCH BACK FOR MIRROR
4 5/8 X 7 5/8

5/8 RADIUS

5/8 RADIUS

19 1/4

7 5/8

3 5/16

4 5/8

7 5/16

FRONT VIEW

1 1/4

5/16   1/4

45°
CHAMFER

11/16

NOTCH
5/16 X
5/16

5/16
5/16

VIEW AT A-A

Finishing

Finish to suit—with the mirror out of the frame—following the general finishing instructions in the introduction. Attach the mirror and backboard using small brads or small square-cut finish nails. I added two picture frame eyebolts with wire to hang the mirror on the wall.

35♦Small Queen Anne Mirror

Not long ago my daughter Jennifer wanted a mirror for her bedroom. I had been through this before with my oldest daughter, Julie, so I already knew I could draw up plans and build one less expensively than I could acquire one. Nevertheless, I did some fresh research and came up with an even dozen designs based on original small antique mirrors that I really liked.

The drawings for this small Queen Anne mirror—and the four mirror projects that follow—represent exact copies of some of the twelve I found in my research.

Instructions

The moulding profile of the top, bottom, and sides of the frame can be made using a combination of router or shaper bits. If you plan to make many mirrors for resale, you might want to have a custom router bit made up. These are not very expensive and will save a lot of time and do a very professional job.

Cut all of the pieces to overall size according to the materials list. Sand all surfaces down with a fine grit of sandpaper—this will save you from having to do a lot of finish sanding later.

Cut the moulding profile shape of the face of the top, bottom, and two sides. (It is a good idea to make a few extra pieces just in case you make an error cutting.) Make the rabbet cut in the back according to the plans for the mirror.

Make exact 45-degree mitre cuts at the ends of the top, bottom, and side pieces as shown in the plans.

Glue the frame together. Be sure to keep all corners at *exactly* 90 degrees. After the glue sets, cut notches for the top, bottom, and side scrolls—as required. Refer carefully to the plans as you make the project.

On a sheet of paper draw a ½-inch grid. Lay out the top, bottom, and side scrolls (as required). Transfer each pattern to the wood.

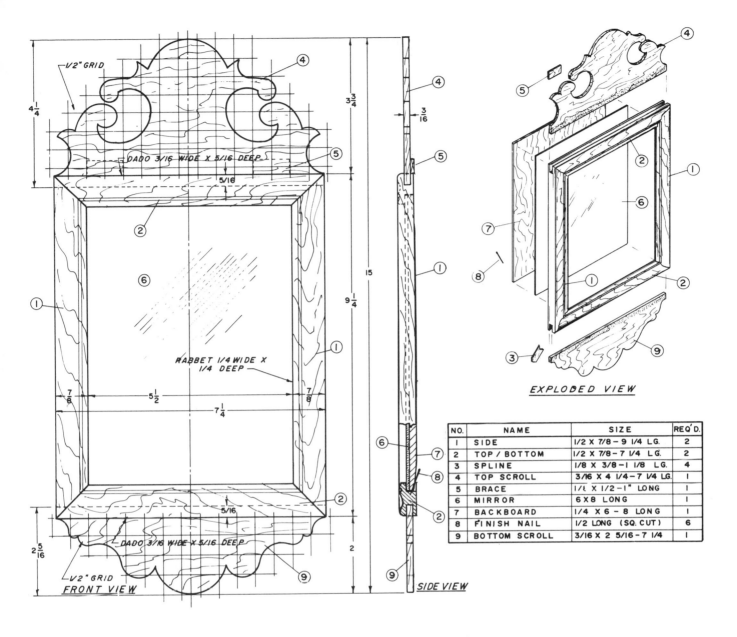

NO.	NAME	SIZE	REQ'D.
1	SIDE	1/2 X 7/8 – 9 1/4 LG.	2
2	TOP / BOTTOM	1/2 X 7/8 – 7 1/4 LG.	2
3	SPLINE	1/8 X 3/8 – 1 1/8 LG.	4
4	TOP SCROLL	3/16 X 4 1/4 – 7 1/4 LG.	1
5	BRACE	1/2 X 1/2 – 1" LONG	1
6	MIRROR	6 X 8 LONG	1
7	BACKBOARD	1/4 X 6 – 8 LONG	1
8	FINISH NAIL	1/2 LONG (SQ. CUT)	6
9	BOTTOM SCROLL	3/16 X 2 5/16 – 7 1/4	1

Important: Before cutting out, check that the distance across the mirror frame is *exactly* the same dimension as your scroll patterns. *This is very important.* Carefully cut out the top and bottom scroll (as required).

All that is left to do now is to glue the scroll(s) to the frame subassembly. After the glue sets, add the brace(s).

Resand all over using very fine sandpaper. Then, cut the backboard to size according to the plans. Sand all over once again.

Finishing

Apply a stain of your choice as you wish. If you use a wood such as walnut, mahogany, or even cherry, you may not want to apply a stain. Apply four or five satin-finish top coats such as tung oil or Watco oil. Lightly sand between coats using 0000 steel wool. Add a coat of paste wax and your mirror frame is ready for the mirror.

Add the mirror and backboard as shown with square-cut finish nails.

Clean and polish the mirror and your wall mirror is ready to sell or hang—perfect for any room.

107

36 ◆ Medium-Size Wall Mirror

Here is a simple mirror project taken from the ones I collected after my daughter Jennifer let me know she wanted a mirror for her bedroom. It is quite different from the preceding Queen Anne mirror, and yet it bears some similarity to the Queen Anne mirror project that follows. To find the right mirror for your needs, you will probably want to look closely at these three, as well as at Projects 38 and 39 that follow. As with any of these mirrors, choose the best wood you can find. This mirror is made in exactly the same way as Project 35. Simply follow the instructions for Project 35 in making and finishing this project.

NO.	NAME	SIZE	REQ'D.
1	SIDE	5/8 X 13/16 – 12 1/8 LG.	2
2	TOP/BOTTOM	5/8 X 13/16 – 10 LONG	2
3	SPLINE	1/8 X 5/16 – 1 LONG	4
4	TOP SCROLL	1/4 X 5 1/2 – 10 LONG	1
5	BRACE	1/4 X 3/4 – 2 LONG	2
6	MIRROR	8 7/8 X 11 LONG	1
7	BACKBOARD	1/4 X 8 7/8 – 11 LG.	1
8	FINISH NAIL	3/4 LONG (SQ. CUT)	6

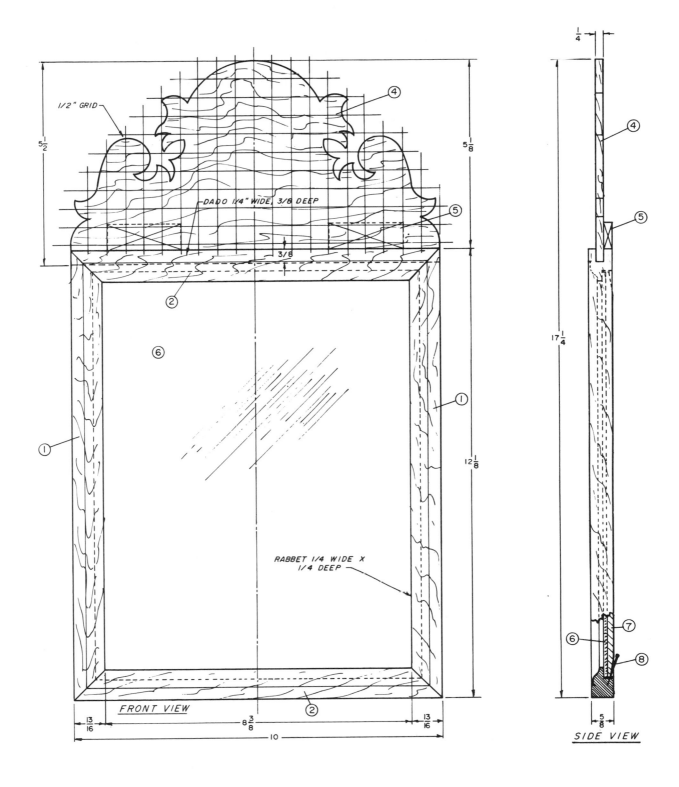

1/2" GRID

5 1/2

DADO 1/4" WIDE, 3/8 DEEP

④

5 5/8

⑤

3/8

②

⑥

17 1/4

①

①

12 1/8

RABBET 1/4 WIDE X
1/4 DEEP

FRONT VIEW

②

13/16

8 3/8

②

13/16

10

1/4

④

⑤

⑥

⑦

⑧

5/8

SIDE VIEW

109

37 ◆ Queen Anne Wall Mirror

Here is a slightly larger Queen Anne wall mirror than offered in Project 35. Even though this mirror is completely different in size and shape, it is made and assembled exactly the same way. Simply follow the instructions for Project 35 in making and finishing this project. As noted earlier, a mirror such as this can be sold for a very good price—this makes a great project for resale.

NO.	NAME	SIZE	REQ'D.
1	SIDE	3/4 X 1 1/8 – 13 LG.	2
2	TOP BOTTOM	3/4 X 1 1/8 – 8 5/8 LG.	2
3	SPLINE	1/8 X 1/2 – 1 1/4 LG.	4
4	TOP SCROLL	5/16 X 6 – 9 LONG	1
5	BRACE	1/4 X 3/4 –1 LONG	3
6	GLASS	6 7/8 X 11 1/4 LG.	1
7	BACKBOARD	1/4 X 6 7/8– 11 1/4	1
8	FINISH NAIL	3/4 LG. (SQ. CUT)	6

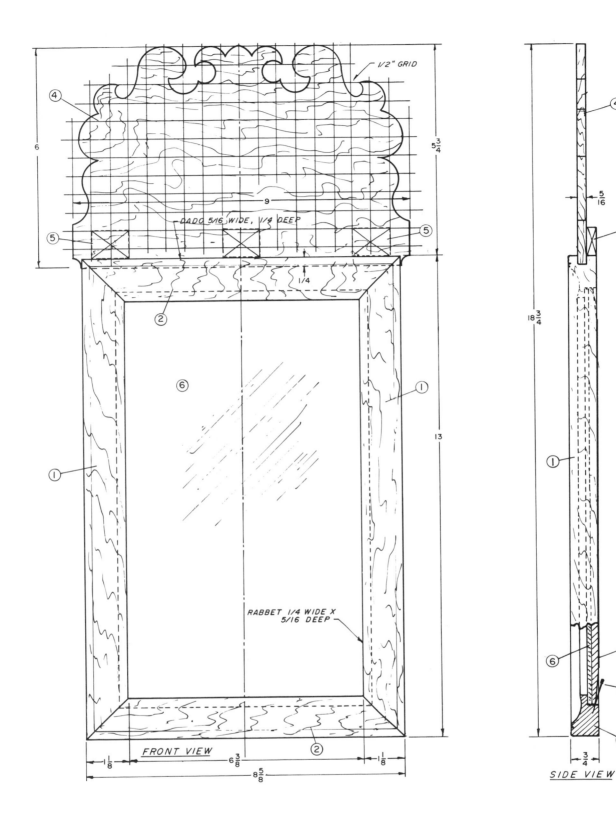

Note: The plans show the original moulding; I chose to use the tools and bits I had handy, so the moulding in my version (photograph) varies slightly.

38 ♦ Long Chippendale Wall Mirror

This mirror and the large Chippendale wall mirror that follows have somewhat more decoration to them than Projects 35, 36, and 37. Nevertheless, they are made in exactly the same way. Simply follow the instructions for Project 35 in making and finishing this project.

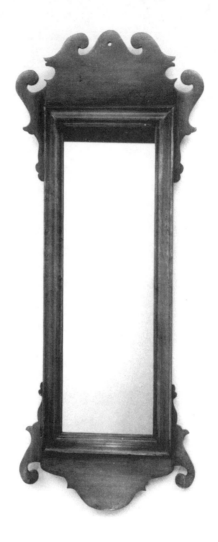

The Chippendale period, as we now designate it, was from 1750 to 1785. The name derives from Thomas Chippendale of London, England, whose book of 1754 titled *The Gentleman and Cabinet Maker's Directory* widely popularized the furniture style characterized by graceful outline and ornate or elaborate ornamentation. It was the most complete and comprehensive furniture manual that had ever been published. The book provided inspiration for craftsmen in the American colony as well as in many other countries throughout the world.

NO.	NAME	SIZE	REQ'D.	NO.	NAME	SIZE	REQ'D.
1	SIDE	3/4 X 7/8 - 18 3/8 LG.	2	6	MIRROR	5 3/8 X 17 1/8 LG.	1
2	TOP/BOTTOM	3/4 X 7/8 - 6 5/8 LG.	2	7	BACKBOARD	1/4 X 5 3/8 - 17 1/8 LG.	1
3	SPLINE	1/4 X 3/4 - 1" LONG	4	8	FINISH NAIL	3/4 LONG (SQ. CUT)	8
4	TOP SCROLL	1/4 X 4 1/4 - 9 5/8 LG.	1	9	BOTTOM SCROLL	1/4 X 3 1/8 - 9 1/8 LG.	1
4A	TOP SIDE SCROLL	1/4 X 1 3/4 - 5 13/16	2	9A	BOTTOM SIDE SCROLL	1/4 X 1 1/2 - 5 5/16 LG.	2
5	BRACE	1/4 X 1/2 - 1 1/2 LG.	2				

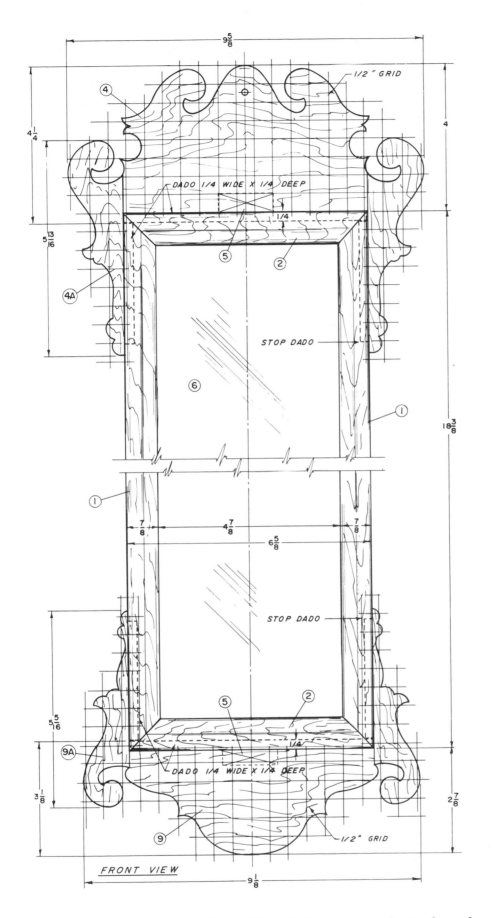

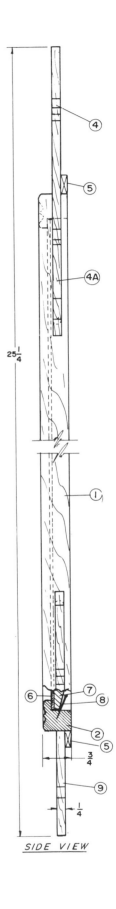

Note: The plans show the original moulding; I chose to use the tools and bits I had handy, so the moulding in my version (photograph) varies slightly.

39◆Large Chippendale Wall Mirror

Here is the last mirror I'm including from the dozen I researched after my daughter said she wanted one for her bedroom. I think that you will be able to find one or two that you want to make. I made all twelve, but this I liked the most. Again, simply follow the instructions for Project 35 in making and finishing this project.

NO.	NAME	SIZE	REQ'D.
1	SIDE	3/4 X 1 1/4 - 25 1/4	2
2	TOP / BOTTOM	3/4 X 1 1/4 - 17 1/4	2
3	SPLINE	1/8 X 1 3/8 - 2 1/2	4
4	TOP SCROLL	3/8 X 10 - 17 1/4 LG.	1
5	TOP SIDE SCROLL	3/8 X 2 1/8 - 8 LG.	2
6	BOTTOM SCROLL	3/8 X 5 5/8 - 17 1/4	1
7	BOTTOM SIDE SCROLL	3/8 X 2 1/2 - 7 1/2	2
8	BRACE	1/4 X 3/4 - 2 1/2	10
9	MIRROR	3/32 X 15 1/4 - 23 1/4	1
10	BACKBOARD	1/4 X 15 1/4 - 23 1/4	1
11	FINISH NAIL	3/4 LONG	8

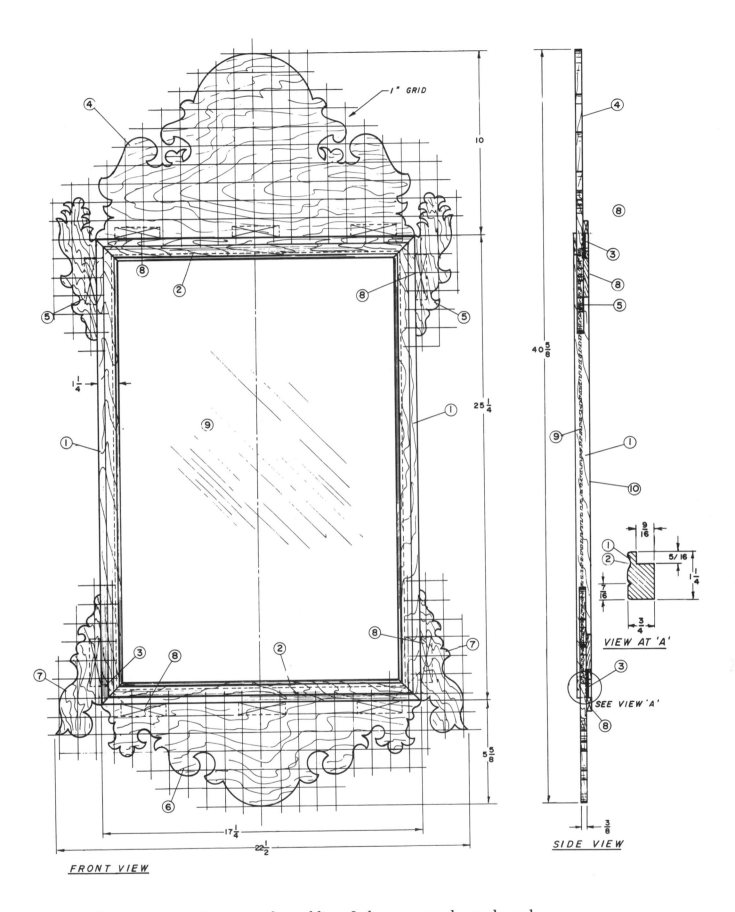

FRONT VIEW

VIEW AT 'A'

SIDE VIEW

Note: The plans show the original moulding; I chose to use the tools and bits I had handy, so the moulding in my version (photograph) varies slightly.

115

CLOCK PROJECTS

40 ◆ Shaker Shelf Clock, circa 1850

I have a collection of original clocks—most of which have wooden works. Clocks are among my favorite antiques—some of the most beautiful were made by the Shakers. I don't think I've seen an original Shaker clock for sale that I can recall; most are found in museums. The three of four models that I especially like were made by Isaac Benjamin Youngs from Watervliet, New York. This is his third model that I have recorded (a fourth is Project 43). The others I drew full-size; this one has been scaled down to 50 percent of the original.

The original was very large—much too large for today's homes. I have kept the same lines and proportions. This one was made of cherry wood around 1850 or so. Except for the door, this is a very simple clock to make. Note that the clock hands and face shown in the plans reproduce the original, while my copy (photograph) reflects the elements I could locate that were still in keeping with the original.

A religious sect called the United Society of Believers in Christ's Second Appearing started in England around 1706. Because of their quivering and shaking during religious service, they became known as the Shakers. They believed that their furniture was originally designed in heaven and that the patterns were transmitted to them by angels; thus, their products had to be perfectly made, free from all blemishes. By 1840 there were about twenty colonies in the United States, from Maine to Indiana. Shakers were well known for their fine furniture and products.

The Shaker elders were allowed to carry watches, but, for everyone else, such watches were considered an indulgence and unnecessary. Clocks, on the other hand, were indispensable and did not have the restrictions watches had.

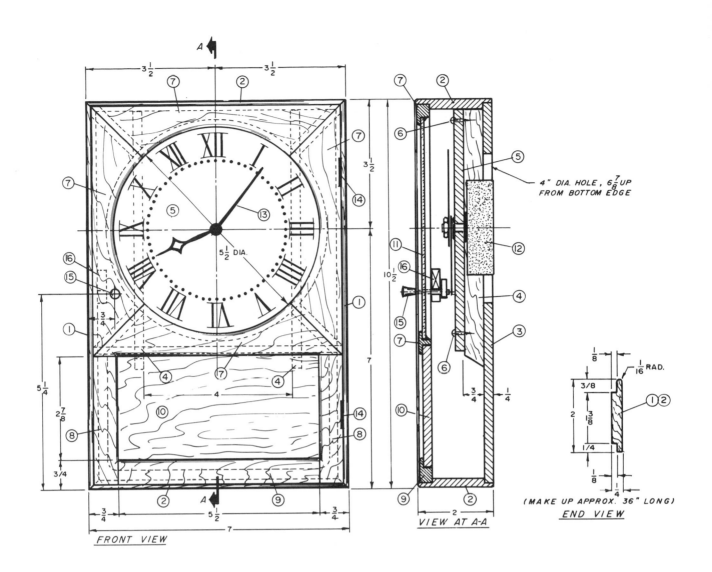

FRONT VIEW

VIEW AT A-A

4" DIA. HOLE, 6 7/8 UP FROM BOTTOM EDGE

5 1/2 DIA.

(MAKE UP APPROX. 36" LONG)
END VIEW

1/16 RAD.

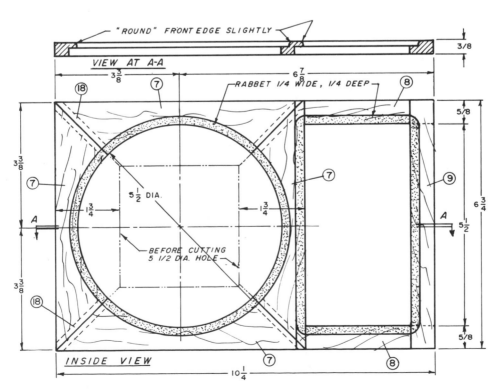

"ROUND" FRONT EDGE SLIGHTLY

VIEW AT A-A

RABBET 1/4 WIDE, 1/4 DEEP

5 1/2 DIA.

BEFORE CUTTING
5 1/2 DIA. HOLE

INSIDE VIEW

117

NO.	NAME	SIZE	REQ'D.
1	SIDE	1/4 X 2 - 10 1/2 LG.	2
2	TOP / BOTTOM	1/4 X 2 - 7 LONG	2
3	BACK (PINE)	1/4 X 6 3/4 - 10 1/4	1
4	DIAL SUPPORT	1/4 X 3/4 - 7 LG.	2
5	DIAL FACE	1/4 X 6 1/2 X 6 1/2	1
6	SCREW RD. HD.	NO. 6 - 3/4 LONG	4
7	DOOR SEGMENT	3/8 X 1 3/4 - 6 3/4	4
8	DOOR SIDE	3/8 X 5/8 - 3 1/2 LG.	2
9	DOOR BOTTOM	3/8 X 5/8 - 5 1/2 LG.	1
10	PANEL	1/4 X 3 1/4 - 6 LG.	1
11	GLASS	6 DIA.	1
12	MOVEMENT	QUARTZ	1
13	HANDS	2 1/4 SIZE	1 PR.
14	HINGE	3/4 W - 5/8 H	2
15	KNOB W/ LATCH	MAKE FROM SCRAP	1
16	BLOCK FOR LATCH	TO SUIT	1
17	DIAL FACE	3 3/4 TIME RING.	1
18	SPLINE	1/16 X 1/4 - 1 3/4	4

Instructions

Study the plans carefully. Note how each part is to be shaped. As you study the plans, try to *visualize* how you will make each part and how the project will be assembled. Note which parts you will put together first, second, and so on—exactly how *you* will put it together.

I recommend that you make the door assembly first and build the box case around the door.

The wood will have to be planed down to ¼-inch thickness, if you can't purchase it at the correct thickness. Because the clock is scaled down, the wood ended up as ¼-inch thick.

Carefully cut all of the parts to size according to the materials list. Take care to cut all parts to exact size and exactly square (90 degrees). *Stop and recheck all dimensions before going on.*

Lightly sand all surfaces and edges with medium sandpaper to remove all tool marks. Take care to keep *all* edges square and sharp.

Make the door following the plans; except, make the door solid without the round 5½-inch-diameter cutout. Cut out the hole *after* the door is made. For strength—even though I doubt the scaled-down version needs it—add splines, parts number 18, to hold the three door segments, parts number 7, together.

Note: I suggest cutting an extra door segment, part number 7, in case you have trouble getting a good fit.

Refer to the exploded view—note how the bottom of the door is notched to hold it all together. The panel, part number 10, actually adds strength to the bottom section of the door.

Carefully make up the door to the approximate sizes given. After the glue sets, sand the top and bottom surfaces—especially the front surface. Locate and cut out the 5½-inch-diameter hole, as shown. Using a router and a rabbet cutter with a follower, make the rabbet cuts on the *inside* surface, as illustrated on the drawing. Note that the *inside* view is given. Turn the door over and "round" the front surface of the 5½-inch-diameter edge, as shown—approximately ⅟₁₆ inch or so.

Resand all over, and sand the four edges of the door assembly at this time, keeping the edges sharp and square.

The hard part is over; all that is left is to make a simple four-piece box to go around the door.

Carefully cut the profile of the top, bottom, and sides, parts number 1 and 2. Mitre the top, bottom, and side pieces to length, cut at *exactly* 45 degrees. Assemble the box. Cut and fit the back, part number 3, to the case.

Make the dial supports and the dial face, parts number 4 and 5. Locate and glue the dial supports in place, approximately 4 inches apart. Temporarily, attach the dial face to the supports with small screws, parts number 6.

Fit the door assembly to the case with the two brass hinges, parts number 14. Because the side panel, part number 1, is *so* thin where the hinge is attached, I attached the hinges to the door and then epoxied them to the sides. (This was *so* quick and easy that I think I will use this technique on more projects.) Use a thin piece of paper between the leaves of the hinges so any epoxy that gets on the other leaf will not glue the hinge together.

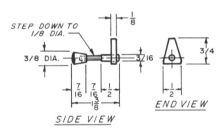

Make up the latch assembly and the block for the latch, parts number 15 and 16, out of scrap wood pieces, as shown. Check that it works correctly, locking the door shut—adjust as necessary. I fitted these pieces *before* attaching the backboard in place.

Glue the dial face paper, part number 17, to the board, part number 5, positioning it in the *center* of the 5½-inch hole in the door—this is important. Remove the dial face and drill the hole for the movement, part number 12.

Add the glass, part number 11, using black putty, if you can find it.

Finishing

Finish to suit, following the general finishing instructions in the introduction—a clear satin top coat would be best.

Attach the movement to the dial face; add a battery and the hands according to the instructions that came with the movement. Attach the dial face to the supports using the four wood screws. Your reproduction will be enjoyed for the next 150 years.

41◆Square New England Wall Clock, circa 1800

This original clock is simply a frame with a porcelain dial face. It was made around 1800. Porcelain faces can be purchased today; so, this project is very easy to make.

Instructions

Study the plans carefully.

Make up material for the frame and trim, parts number 1 and 2. The frame's profile is given in the *Frame Detail* on the plans. Make up about 72 inches of this material. Measure and mitre the four frame pieces, cut at 45 degrees and at exactly the same length as given in the plans. Cut a saw kerf along the 45-degree cut for the spline—this will give the frame a lot of added strength. Glue the frame pieces together with the splines, parts number 3.

Note: *It is a good idea to have the porcelain dial face before cutting the frame lengths. Fit the frame to the dial face.*

Attach the trim pieces, parts number 2, around the frame. Let them overhang the frame about 3/16 inch, as shown in the view at A–A.

Finishing

Finish to suit, following the general finishing instructions in the introduction. Attach the dial face, part number 4, with the four inserts, parts number 5. Attach the movement, part number 6, to the dial. Add the hands and a fresh battery. The movement provides a built-in hanger.

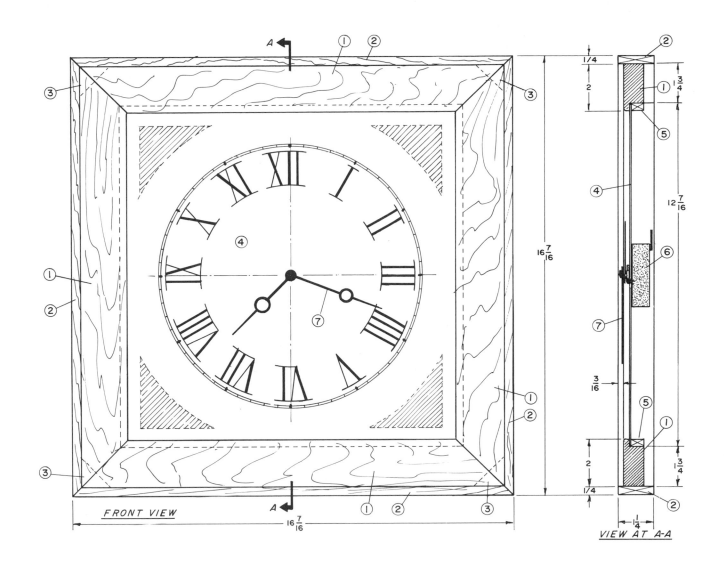

FRONT VIEW

16 7/16

VIEW AT A-A

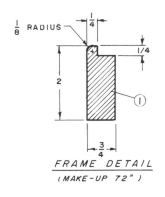

1/8 RADIUS

FRAME DETAIL
(MAKE-UP 72")

NO.	NAME	SIZE	REQ'D.
1	FRAME	3/4 X 2 - 15 15/16 LG.	4
2	TRIM	1/4 X 1 1/4 - 16 7/16	4
3	SPLINE	1/8 X 3/4 - 1 1/4 LG.	4
4	DIAL FACE (METAL)	9 1/2 TIME RING	1
5	INSERT	1/4 X 1/2 - 12 7/16	4
6	MOVEMENT	QUARTZ	1
7	MOON HANDS	4 3/4 SIZE	1 PR.

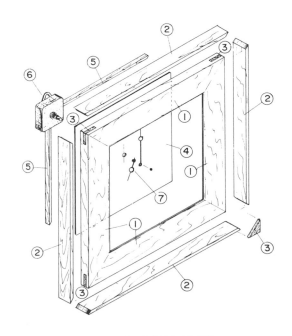

EXPLODED VIEW

121

42 ◆ Formal Wall Clock

If you want a "formal" look for a room, this clock is for you. Except for the front panel assembly, it is as simple as making a box!

This project should be made of a fine hardwood—I recommend mahogany or walnut. The original was made of solid walnut. I like walnut because it gives such a pleasing finish. Selecting the finest materials you can is always worth the effort and expense for a project such as this. Note that the clock hands and face shown in the plans reproduce the original, while my copy (photograph) reflects the elements I could locate that were still in keeping with the original. I like to draw my own dial faces using the purchased paper dial as a pattern. The original faces were hand-painted, but you can use draftsman's ink to draw your dial face.

Instructions

Study the plans carefully. Note how each part is to be shaped. As you study the plans, try to *visualize* how you will make each part and how the project will be assembled. Note which parts you will put together first, second, and so on—exactly how *you* will put it together.

The scroll top, part number 9, is the only irregular shape on the clock and will have to be laid out on a ½-inch grid to make the full-size pattern.

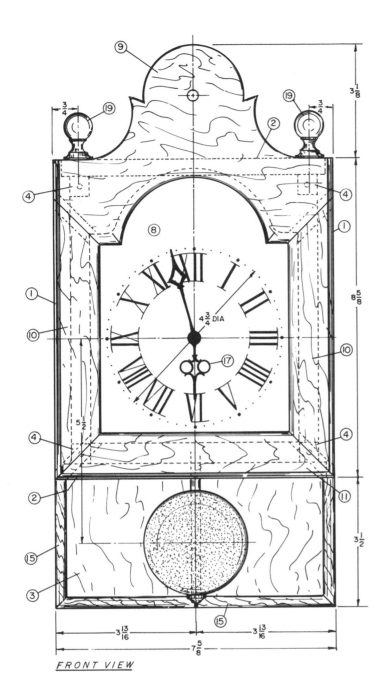

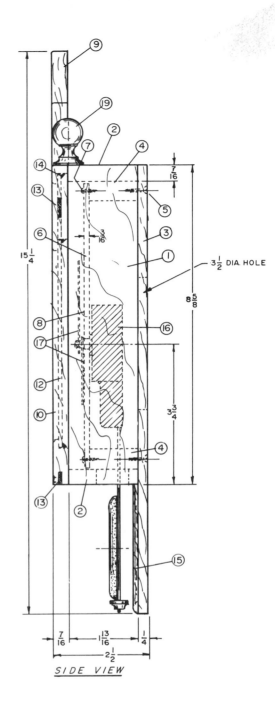

FRONT VIEW

SIDE VIEW

Lay out the grid on heavy paper or cardboard, and transfer the shape of the piece to the grid, point by point.

Transfer the full-size pattern to the wood, and carefully cut out the piece. Check all dimensions for accuracy. Sand all over with fine grit sandpaper, keeping all edges sharp.

Carefully cut the remaining parts to size according to the materials list. Take care to cut the parts to exact size and exactly square (90 degrees). *Stop and recheck all dimensions before going on.*

Lightly sand all surfaces and edges with medium sandpaper to remove all tool marks. Take care to keep *all* edges square and sharp.

Make up the box assembly using parts number 1, 2, 3, 4, and 5. The top, bottom, and sides are glued together—the other parts are screwed in place. Be sure to cut out a ⅞-inch by 6⅜-inch slot in the bottom piece for the pendulum.

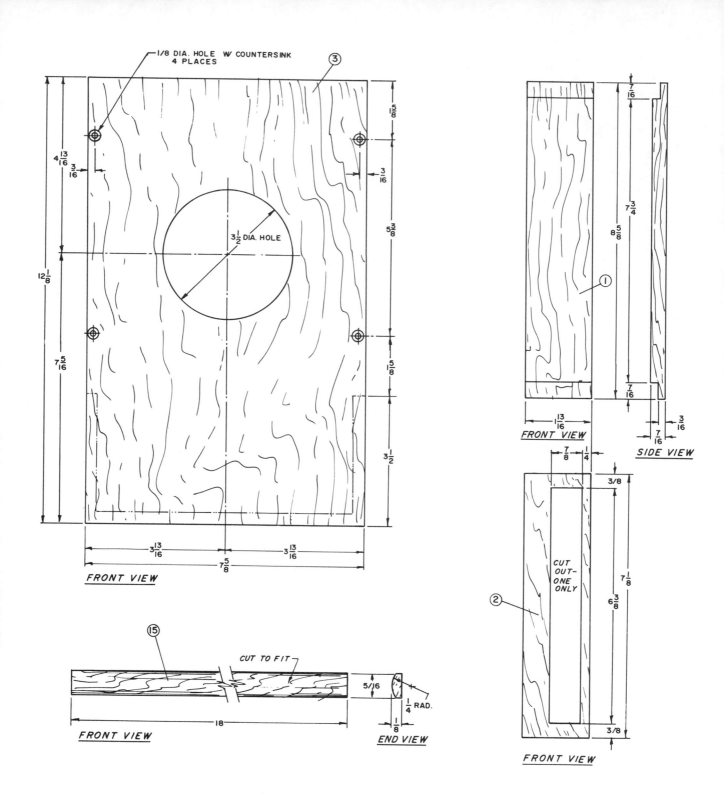

Note: The backboard, part number 3, is screwed in place, not glued—this is so you can get to the movement, if necessary.

Assemble the backboard, part number 3, to the box assembly using the wood screws. Fit the half-round mouldings, parts number 15, using 45-degree mitre cuts, as shown. Remove the backboard.

Make up the front assembly using the scroll top, sides, and bottom pieces, parts number 9, 10, 11, and 13. After all of the pieces have been carefully made, dry-fit the parts. If all parts fit together correctly, assemble the project, keeping everything square as you go. Check that all fits are tight.

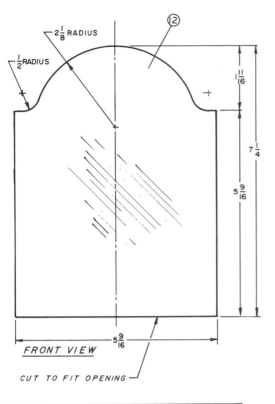

FRONT VIEW

CUT TO FIT OPENING

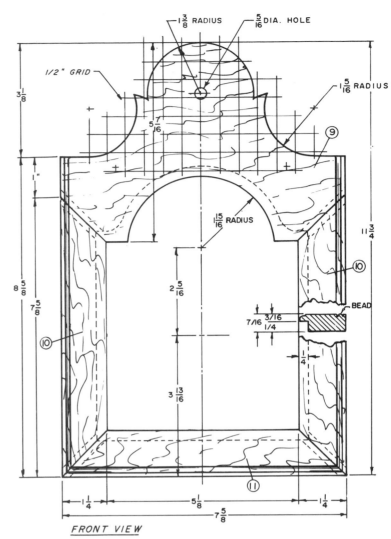

FRONT VIEW

NO.	NAME	SIZE	REQ'D.
1	SIDE	7/16 X 1 13/16 – 8 5/8 LG.	2
2	TOP / BOTTOM	7/16 X 1 13/16 – 7 1/8 LG.	2
3	BACK BOARD	1/4 X 7 5/8 – 12 1/8 LG.	1
4	BLOCK	1/2 X 1/2 – 1 1/4 LG.	4
5	SCREW – FL. HD.	NO. 6 – 5/8 LONG	4
6	DIAL FACE SUPPORT	3/16 X 6 3/4 – 7 3/4	1
7	SCREW – RD. HD.	NO. 6 – 1/2 LONG	4
8	DIAL FACE	4 1/2 DIA	1
9	SCROLL TOP	7/16 X 5 7/16 – 7 5/8	1
10	SIDE	7/16 X 1 1/4 – 7 5/8	2
11	BOTTOM	7/16 X 1 1/4 – 7 5/8	1
12	GLASS	3/32 X 5 9/16 – 7 1/4	1
13	SPLINE	1/8 X 1/4 – 1 3/4 LG.	4
14	PUTTY BLACK	–	AS REQ'D
15	MOLDING	1/8 X 5/16 – 18 LG.	1
16	QUARTZ · MOVEMENT		1
17	HANDS (4 1/2)		1 PR.
18	SCREW – FL. HD.	NO. 6 X 7/8 LONG	4
19	BRASS BALL	3/4 DIA.	2

After the glue sets, cut the bead around the two sides and bottom edges, as shown.

Using a router and a rabbet cutter with a ball-bearing follower, cut the inside rabbet for the glass. (This completes the hard part.)

Add the glass to the front assembly using black putty, if you can find it. Take care to "round" the sharp corners on the glass when you are cutting it; this should also stop it from splitting where you don't want it to.

Glue the front assembly to the box assembly. Attach the dial face, part number 8, to the dial face support board, part number 6, using rubber cement.

Attach the four blocks, parts number 4, to the backboard, part number 3, as shown, using four wood screws. Attach the dial face support, part number 6, using four wood screws. This will form a subassembly that can be taken apart later, if necessary, to add a battery or to remove the movement.

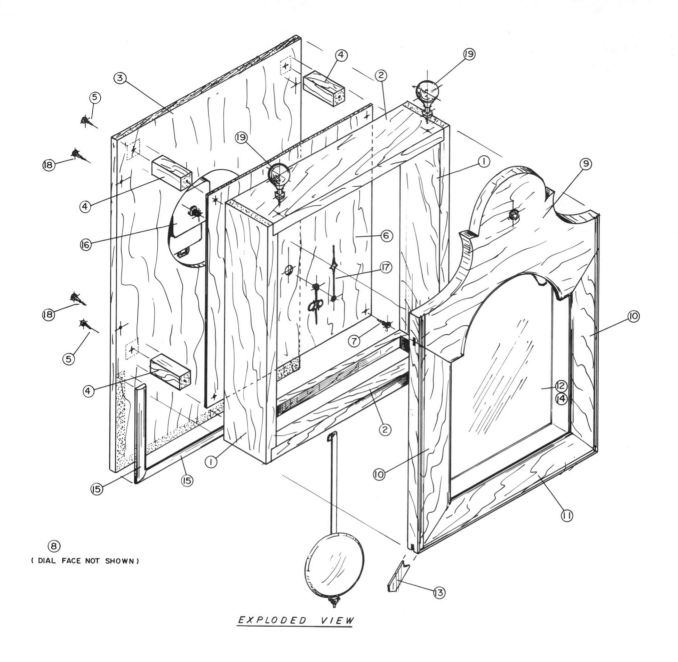

(8)
(DIAL FACE NOT SHOWN)

EXPLODED VIEW

Finishing

Finish to suit, following the general finishing instructions in the introduction. A satin finish would be best.

Assemble the movement, hands, and battery to the dial face, and reassemble the backboard with the dial face and movement in place. Add the two brass balls and a simple picture frame hanger.

Set your clock, and you're ready to hang it on the wall.

43 ♦ Shaker Wall Clock, circa 1840

This clock is a copy of a clock Isaac Youngs made in 1840 at the age of 47. It was made of pine and had a light exterior stain and a dark-walnut stain interior.

Variations of this wall clock that were also made by Isaac had double glass panels in the lower door in place of the wood panel. I have drawn up the plans and made a copy of the glass door variation, which I have presented in my earlier book, 52 *Weekend Woodworking Projects* (Sterling, 1991). The construction is almost identical, but the finished look of each clock is quite distinct.

Shakers never married or bore children, so their sect was kept alive for a time by the acceptance of converts as new members. This led to the decimation of the sect, especially in combination with the changing economy after the Civil War; handcrafted products could no longer compete with lower-cost, factory-made products.

There were very few Shaker clockmakers—perhaps ten at the most. One of the most famous of these was Isaac Benjamin Youngs from Watervliet, New York. He was born July 2, 1793, and died at the age of 72 in 1865. He became the chief clock maker at the New Lebanon, New York, colony. Although Isaac built tall case clocks, his most well-known clock design is one of a few variations of this small wall clock. This clock was particularly interesting in that the backboard of the clock was also the backplate of the wooden-gear movement. Isaac Youngs was one of the few Shaker craftsmen who wasn't afraid to experiment and to try innovative ideas.

Instructions

Study all of the drawings very carefully; be sure you fully understand how the various parts are made and go together before starting. You will see this wall clock is not much more than a simple box with two lids—doors.

This project goes together quite quickly so you might want to order the parts in plenty of time and not be held up waiting for the purchased parts.

Cut all parts to overall size according to the materials list. Sand the surfaces with medium to fine grit sandpaper.

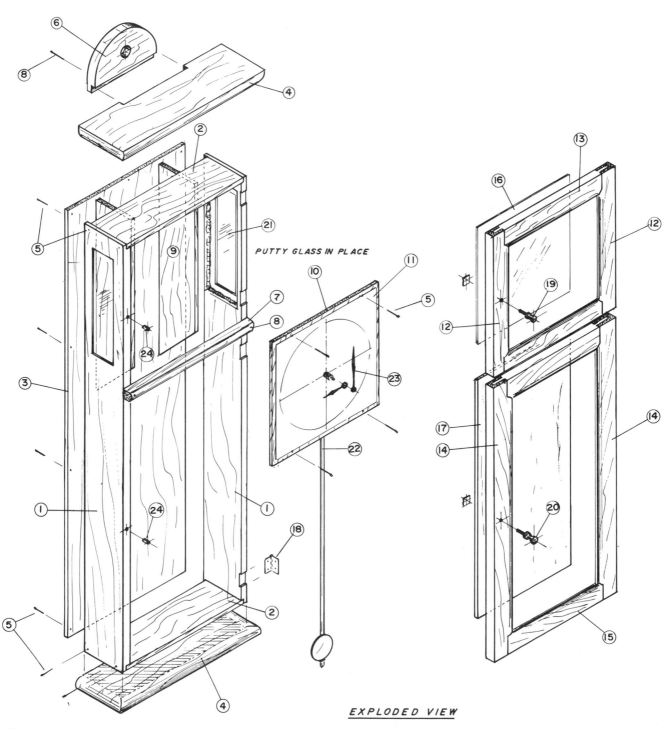

PUTTY GLASS IN PLACE

EXPLODED VIEW

Locate and cut out the 1¾-inch by 7½-inch windows of the two sides, parts number 1. Cut the ¼-inch wide by ¼-inch deep rabbet along the top, back, and bottom surfaces. Notch for the four hinges on the *right* side only. Resand all over, keeping all edges sharp.

Cut a 5/16-inch by 5¼-inch notch in the top only, part number 4, as shown, and "round" the front and two sides.

Cut to shape the hanger, part number 6, divider, part number 7, and the dial supports, parts number 9. Again, resand all parts keeping all edges sharp. Dry-fit the box assembly using the exploded view as a guide with parts number 1 through 8—adjust as necessary. When you are satisfied with the fit, apply very little glue and, for authenticity, use square-cut nails. Temporarily set the divider, part number 7, in place—making adjustments later when doors are added as necessary.

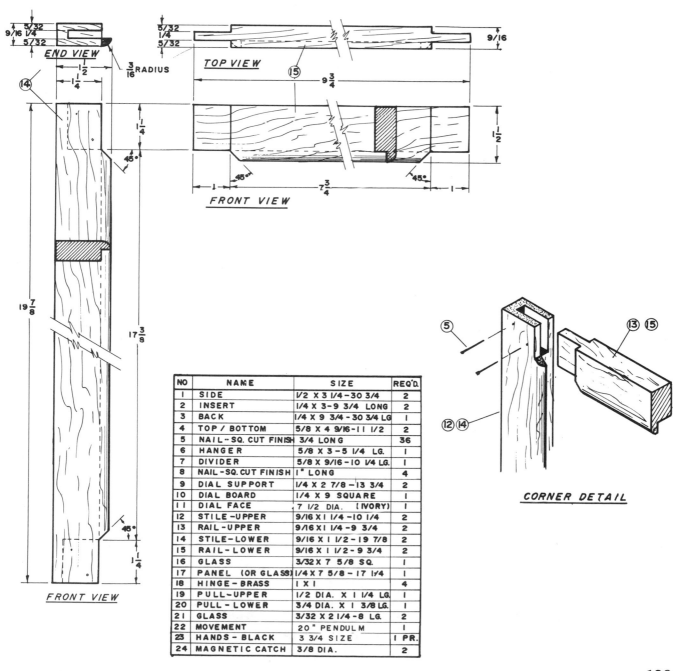

NO	NAME	SIZE	REQ'D.
1	SIDE	1/2 X 3 1/4 - 30 3/4	2
2	INSERT	1/4 X 3 - 9 3/4 LONG	2
3	BACK	1/4 X 9 3/4 - 30 3/4 LG	1
4	TOP / BOTTOM	5/8 X 4 9/16 - 11 1/2	2
5	NAIL - SQ. CUT FINISH	3/4 LONG	36
6	HANGER	5/8 X 3 - 5 1/4 LG.	1
7	DIVIDER	5/8 X 9/16 - 10 1/4 LG.	1
8	NAIL - SQ. CUT FINISH	1" LONG	4
9	DIAL SUPPORT	1/4 X 2 7/8 - 13 3/4	2
10	DIAL BOARD	1/4 X 9 SQUARE	1
11	DIAL FACE	7 1/2 DIA. (IVORY)	1
12	STILE - UPPER	9/16 X 1 1/4 - 10 1/4	2
13	RAIL - UPPER	9/16 X 1 1/4 - 9 3/4	2
14	STILE - LOWER	9/16 X 1 1/2 - 19 7/8	2
15	RAIL - LOWER	9/16 X 1 1/2 - 9 3/4	2
16	GLASS	3/32 X 7 5/8 SQ.	1
17	PANEL (OR GLASS)	1/4 X 7 5/8 - 17 1/4	1
18	HINGE - BRASS	1 X 1	4
19	PULL - UPPER	1/2 DIA. X 1 1/4 LG.	1
20	PULL - LOWER	3/4 DIA. X 1 3/8 LG.	1
21	GLASS	3/32 X 2 1/4 - 8 LG.	2
22	MOVEMENT	20" PENDULM	1
23	HANDS - BLACK	3 3/4 SIZE	1 PR.
24	MAGNETIC CATCH	3/8 DIA.	2

END VIEW

TOP VIEW

FRONT VIEW

3/16 RADIUS

FRONT VIEW

CORNER DETAIL

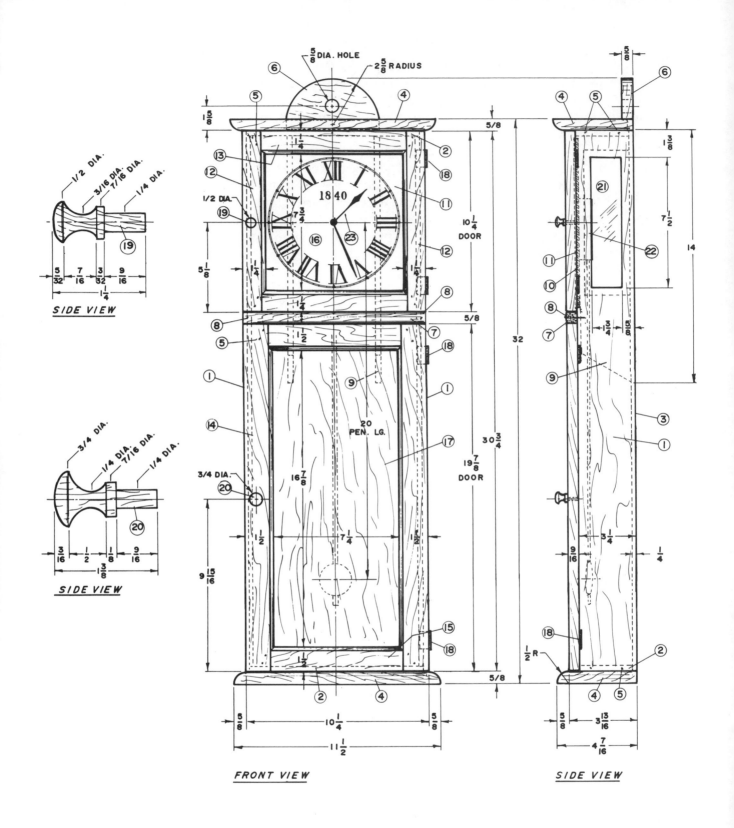

FRONT VIEW

SIDE VIEW

SIDE VIEW

Note: The original clock used a completely different dial face support. In the 1840 clock, the back of the movement was actually the back of the case. The dial face was attached to the movement.

The two dial supports used in this reproduction are the same design as those used in other, wooden weight-driven clocks of the same era.

If you want to see the movement, cut notches in the two dial supports, parts number 9, that line up with the two windows in the sides, parts number

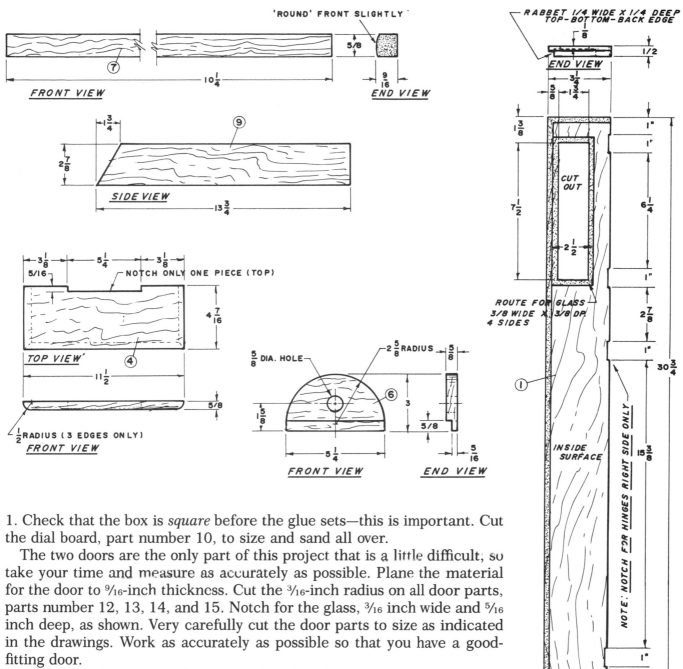

'ROUND' FRONT SLIGHTLY

FRONT VIEW

END VIEW

5/8

9/16

10 1/4

SIDE VIEW

1 3/4

2 7/8

13 3/4

NOTCH ONLY ONE PIECE (TOP)

3 1/8

5 1/4

3 1/8

5/16

4 7/16

TOP VIEW

11 1/2

5/8

1/2 RADIUS (3 EDGES ONLY)

FRONT VIEW

5/8 DIA. HOLE

2 5/8 RADIUS

5/8

3

1 5/8

5 1/4

5/8

5/16

FRONT VIEW

END VIEW

RABBET 1/4 WIDE X 1/4 DEEP TOP-BOTTOM-BACK EDGE

END VIEW

1/8

1/2

3 1/4

5/8

1 1/4

1 3/8

7 1/2

CUT OUT

2 1/2

ROUTE FOR GLASS 3/8 WIDE X 3/8 DP. 4 SIDES

1"

1"

6 1/4

1"

2 7/8

1"

30 3/4

15 3/8

INSIDE SURFACE

NOTE: NOTCH FOR HINGES RIGHT SIDE ONLY

1"

1 1/4

FRONT VIEW

1. Check that the box is *square* before the glue sets—this is important. Cut the dial board, part number 10, to size and sand all over.

The two doors are the only part of this project that is a little difficult, so take your time and measure as accurately as possible. Plane the material for the door to 9/16-inch thickness. Cut the 3/16-inch radius on all door parts, parts number 12, 13, 14, and 15. Notch for the glass, 3/16 inch wide and 5/16 inch deep, as shown. Very carefully cut the door parts to size as indicated in the drawings. Work as accurately as possible so that you have a good-fitting door.

Dry-fit the door parts—also check that they fit with the case correctly. Adjust as necessary. Glue the doors together; for extra strength and for an old "authentic" look, add the square-cut nails, as shown. Do *not* glue the panel, part number 17, in place—let it float.

After the glue sets, fill in any loose joints, and touch up as necessary. Sand all over, keeping all edges sharp. Do not try to hide the nails—they were not hidden on the original clocks. Turn the door pulls, parts number 20, and add them to the doors. Locate and drill for the two round magnetic catches, parts number 24. Make a final fit of the doors, and temporarily add the hinges. Check again that everything fits correctly. Remove the hinges and doors; sand the doors and case using very fine grit sandpaper.

Temporarily attach the two dial supports, parts number 9. They can be tacked or screwed in place from the *back*. Temporarily add the dial board, part number 10. This is held in place by four square-cut, finished nails or small round brass screws.

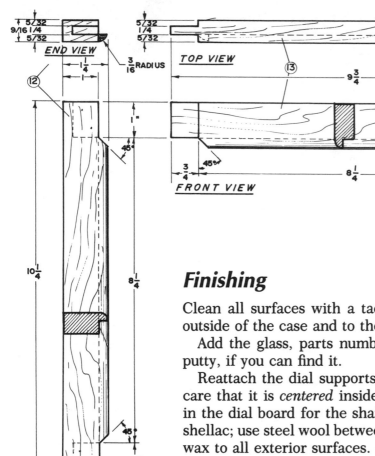

Finishing

Clean all surfaces with a tack rag and apply a coat of pine stain to the outside of the case and to the inside and outside of the two doors.

Add the glass, parts numbers 16 and 21, to the top using a dark grey putty, if you can find it.

Reattach the dial supports. Glue the dial face to the dial board, taking care that it is *centered* inside the *top door*—this is important! Drill a hole in the dial board for the shaft of the movement. Apply two coats of clear shellac; use steel wool between coats with 0000 wool. Apply a coat of paste wax to all exterior surfaces.

Reattach the two doors. Add a battery to the movement, and attach the movement to the dial face with washer and nut. Screw or nail the dial board, with the movement and hands attached, to the dial supports, *with* the movement attached to the face.

Add the pendulum; hang the clock on a peg and give the pendulum a push. Time is on your side—with luck *your* clock will last for 150 years, too.

COUNTRY FURNITURE PROJECTS

44 ♦ "Cricket" Footstool

Footstools were very popular in years gone by. They were found in just about every early Colonial home. Originally they were called "crickets"—although I don't know why. Footstools came in all shapes and sizes. Formal footstools, such as this one, were made of a fine hardwood and usually stained. More "country" footstools were very plain, made of a softwood and usually painted. However, I found an interesting combined treatment in many footstools from Vermont that had stained tops with painted legs and rails.

Instructions

Study the plans carefully. Note how each part is to be shaped. As you study the plans, try to *visualize* how you will make each part and how the project will be assembled. Note which parts you will put together first, second, and so on—exactly how *you* will put it together.

The matching rails, parts number 2, are irregular in shape and will have to be laid out on a 1-inch grid to make a full-size pattern. Lay out the grid on heavy paper or cardboard, and transfer the shape of the piece to the grid, point by point. A compass would come in handy to lay out this pattern.

Transfer the full-size pattern to the wood, and carefully cut out the pieces. Check all dimensions for accuracy. Sand all over with fine grit paper, keeping all edges sharp. I recommend that you tack or tape the two rails together when cutting out and sanding so that your rails will be a perfectly matching pair.

Carefully cut the remaining parts to size according to the materials list. Take care to cut all parts to exact size and exactly square (90 degrees). *Stop and recheck all dimensions before going on.* The top and bottom ends of the legs, parts number 3, are cut at 15 degrees, as shown. Be sure to make one right-hand and one left-hand leg.

NO.	NAME	SIZE	REQ'D.
1	TOP	1/2 X 6 1/2 – 15 LG.	1
2	RAIL	1/2 X 2 1/4 – 13 7/8	2
3	LEG	5/8 X 4 7/8 – 6 1/8	2
4	SQ. CUT FINISH NAIL	1 LONG	18

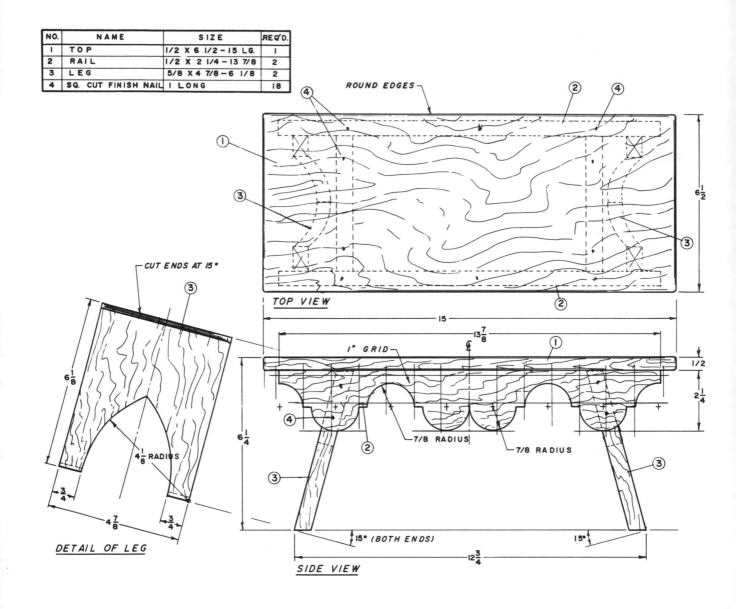

Lightly sand all surfaces and edges with medium sandpaper to remove all tool marks. Take care to keep *all* edges square and sharp.

After all of the pieces have been carefully made, dry-fit the parts—that is, put the complete project together without glue or nails to check for accuracy and good-fitting joints. If anything needs refitting, now is the time to correct it.

Once all of the parts fit together correctly, assemble the project, keeping everything square as you go. Check that all fits are tight. If you used a hardwood, be sure to drill pilot holes for the nails so that the wood will not split.

Finishing

Finish to suit, following the general finishing instructions in the introduction. This project can be stained or painted.

45 ♦ Bed Step Stool

Last year I built my granddaughter Hilary a Colonial pencil-post bed. As with many beds of the period, this one was a little high for a youngster. I knew she had trouble getting in and out of bed; so, when I found this bed step stool in an antique shop in Vermont, I knew it would be just *perfect* for her.

As with many of these country projects, this bed step stool can be used other than for its original purpose. It would be handy anywhere around the house—especially in the kitchen.

Instructions

Study the plans carefully. Note how each part is to be shaped. As you study the plans, try to *visualize* how you will make each part and how the project will be assembled. Note which parts you will put together first, second, and so on—exactly how *you* will put it together.

The two sides, parts number 1, are 14 inches wide; so, if you do not have wood this wide, you will have to glue up wood to make the width. As the sides are irregular in shape they will have to be laid out. If you are going to make only one step stool, lay out the shape directly on the wood. To make a perfectly matching pair, tack the two side pieces together; cut and sand them while they are still tacked together. Locate and cut the two ¾-inch by 1¾-inch notches before separating the parts.

Carefully cut the remaining parts to size according to the materials list. Take care to cut all parts to exact size and exactly square (90 degrees). *Stop and recheck all dimensions before going on.*

Lightly sand all surfaces and edges with medium sandpaper to remove all tool marks. Take care to keep *all* edges square and sharp.

After all of the pieces have been carefully made, dry-fit the parts—that is, put the complete project together without glue or nails to check for accuracy and good-fitting joints. If anything needs refitting, now is the time to correct it.

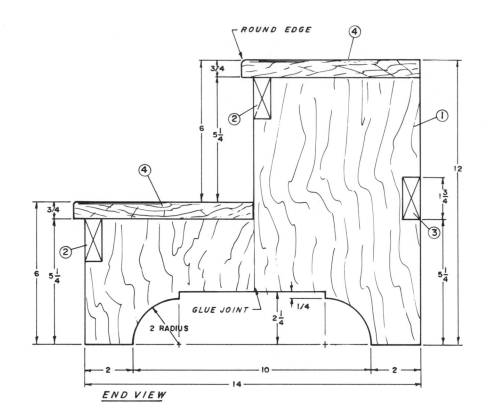

END VIEW

NO.	NAME	SIZE	REQ'D.
1	END	3/4 X 14 –11 1/4 LG.	2
2	FRONT BRACE	3/4 X 1 3/4 –18 LG.	2
3	REAR BRACE	3/4 X 1 3/4 – 18 LG.	1
4	STEP	3/4 X 7 1/2 – 19 LG.	2
5	FINISH NAIL	6 d	24

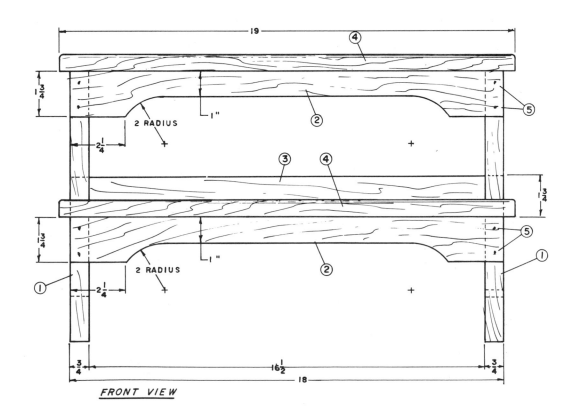

FRONT VIEW

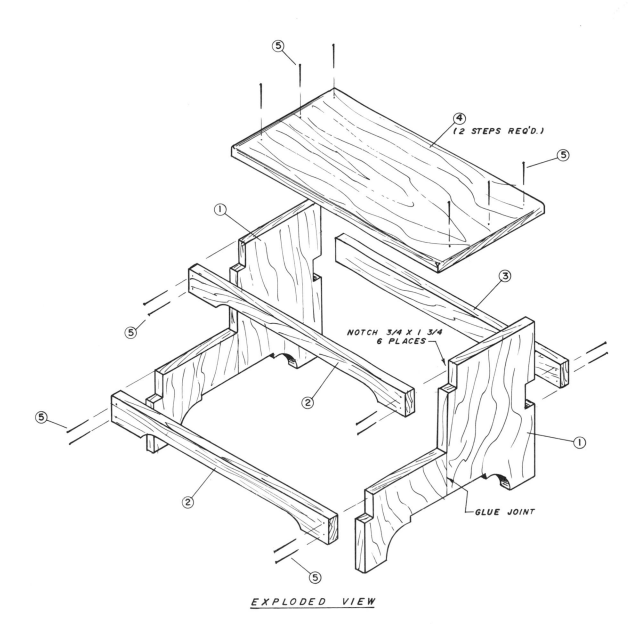

⑤

④
(2 STEPS REQ'D.)

⑤

①

③

⑤

NOTCH 3/4 X 1 3/4
6 PLACES

②

①

②

⑤

GLUE JOINT

⑤

EXPLODED VIEW

Once all of the parts fit together correctly, assemble the project, keeping everything square as you go. Check that all fits are tight.

Finishing

Finish to suit, following the general finishing instructions in the introduction.

46 ◆ Country Bench

This bench is *really* a "Plain Jane"; but in being *so* plain, it has tremendous character. Some genuine antique benches like this—especially Shaker—are quite sought after and valuable. I hadn't had mine finished four days, and someone wanted to buy it. This is a great project for "crackle" paint—or distressing with at *least* two layers of color.

Instructions

Study the plans carefully. Note how each part is to be shaped. As you study the plans, try to *visualize* how you will make each part and how the project will be assembled. Note which parts you will put together first, second, and so on—exactly how *you* will put it together.

Carefully cut all of the parts to size according to the materials list. Take care to cut all parts to exact size and exactly square (90 degrees). *Stop and recheck all dimensions before going on.*

Lightly sand all surfaces and edges with medium sandpaper to remove all tool marks. Take care to keep *all* edges square and sharp.

After all of the pieces have been carefully made, dry-fit the parts—that is, put the complete project together without glue or nails to check for accuracy and good-fitting joints. If anything needs refitting, now is the time to correct it.

Once all of the parts fit together correctly, assemble the project, keeping everything square as you go. Check that all fits are tight.

Finishing

Finish to suit, following the general finishing instructions in the introduction.

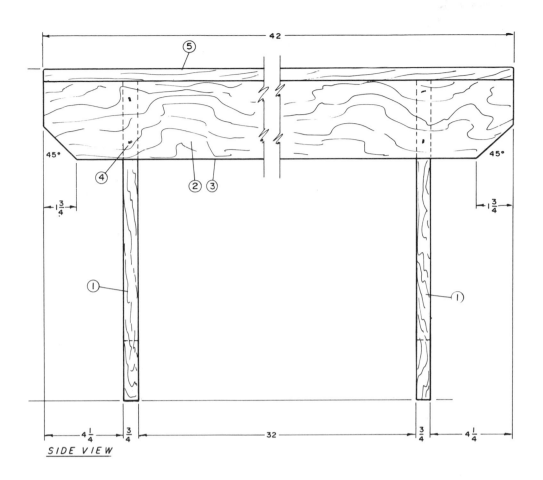

42

⑤

45°   45°

$1\frac{3}{4}$ $1\frac{3}{4}$

④   ②③

①   ①

$4\frac{1}{4}$ $\frac{3}{4}$ 32 $\frac{3}{4}$ $4\frac{1}{4}$

SIDE VIEW

NO.	NAME	SIZE	REQ'D.
1	END	3/4 X 11 1/2 - 17 1/4	2
2	SKIRT	3/4 X 4 1/4 - 42 LG.	2
3	INNER BRACE	3/4 X 4 1/4 - 32 LG.	2
4	SQUARE CUT NAIL	1 1/2 LONG	24
5	TOP	3/4 X 13 1/4 - 42 LG.	1

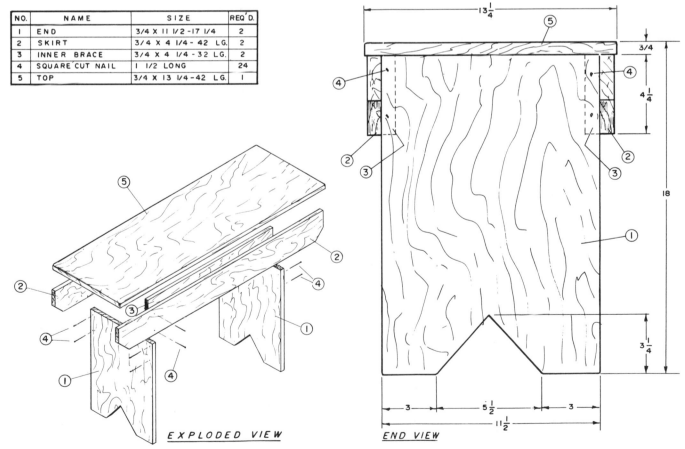

EXPLODED VIEW

$13\frac{1}{4}$

⑤

$\frac{3}{4}$

④   ④

$4\frac{1}{4}$

②   ②

③   ③

①

18

$3\frac{1}{4}$

3      $5\frac{1}{2}$ 3

$11\frac{1}{2}$

END VIEW

139

47♦Square Blanket Chest

I found this chest in a museum in southern Massachusetts, and I liked it the minute I saw it. What especially struck me was that it was so different from most blanket chests of the time. Most blanket chests of the day are *not* square in shape and most did *not* have turned legs; so with all this, I just had to have it. I took notes and a few overall measurements along with three or four photographs of it so I could recall the details. You will need a lathe to make the legs. I really like the wooden hinges, parts number 4.

Instructions

Study the plans carefully. Note how each part is to be shaped. As you study the plans, try to *visualize* how you will make each part and how the project will be assembled. Note which parts you will put together first, second, and so on—exactly how *you* will put it together.

The wooden hinge pieces, parts number 4, are irregular in shape and will have to be laid out. As this is an uncomplicated pattern, simply lay out the shape directly on the wood. Cut both pieces out at the same time by tacking them together. Locate and drill the ⅜-inch-diameter hole in the end while the pieces are still together so that they will be exactly the same.

Cut the remaining parts to overall size according to the materials list. Take care to cut all parts to exact size and exactly square (90 degrees). *Stop and recheck all dimensions before going on.*

Carefully lay out the dovetail tails and pins following the dimensions on the front view. Study the exploded view to see exactly how the dovetail joints are made and assembled. Draw the tails and pins directly on the wood, and cut them out—try to get a tight fit if you can. If they don't turn out perfectly, don't worry—there is always wood filler. (I'm no stranger to wood filler; that's for sure.)

Lightly sand all surfaces and edges with medium sandpaper to remove all tool marks. Take care to keep *all* edges square and sharp.

After all of the pieces have been carefully made, dry-fit the parts—that is, put the complete project together without glue or nails to check for accuracy and good-fitting joints. If anything needs refitting, now is the time to correct it. Be sure to "round" the top, back surface of the backboard so that the lid can open (slide) over and past the backboard.

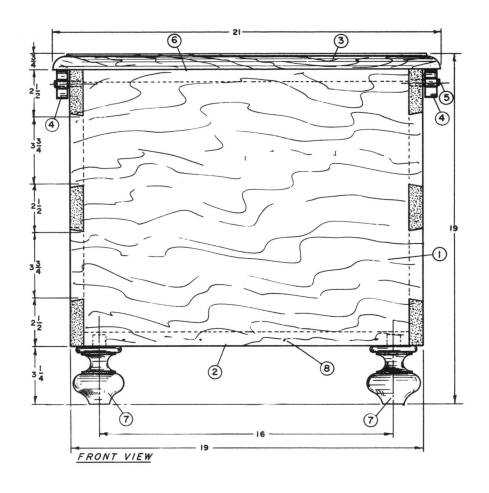

FRONT VIEW

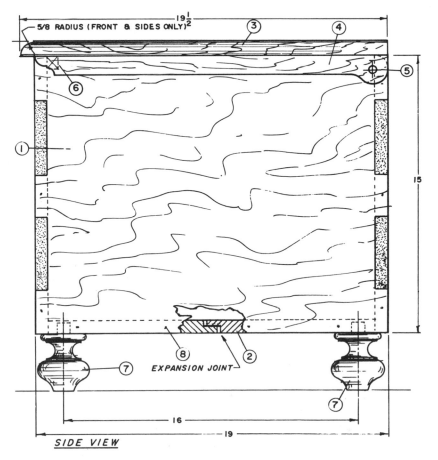

5/8 RADIUS (FRONT & SIDES ONLY)

EXPANSION JOINT

SIDE VIEW

141

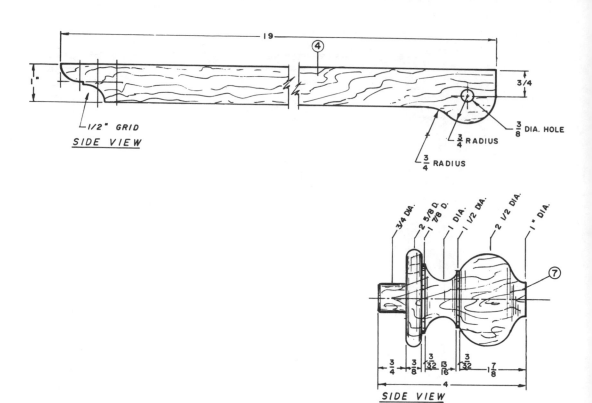

NO.	NAME	SIZE	REQ'D.
1	SIDE	3/4 X 15 - 19 LONG	4
2	BOTTOM	3/4 X 9 1/4-17 1/2 LG.	2
3	TOP (LID)	3/4 X 19 1/2-21 LG.	1
4	HINGE	5/8 X 1 1/2-19 LG.	2
5	HINGE PIN	3/8 DIA. X 1 1/2 LG.	2
6	DUST LIP	3/4 X 1-17 1/2 LG.	1
7	LEG	2 5/8 DIA.-6 LONG	4
8	SQ. CUT NAIL	1 3/4 LONG	AS REQ'D.

Cut the ⅝-inch radius around the two sides and front edges of the lid, part number 3, as shown. *Do not "round" the back edge of the lid.*

Locate and drill for the four legs in the bottom surface.

Once all of the parts fit together correctly, assemble the project keeping everything square as you go. Check that all fits are tight.

Note: The bottom boards, parts number 2, are loosely fit where they join, to allow for expansion of the wide bottom.

Turn the box over and center it on top of the lid, keeping the back of the box and the back of the lid flush. Mark the two sides and front on the bottom of the lid to locate where the hinges should be placed. Leave a ¹⁄₁₆-inch space between the box assembly and hinges.

Add a little glue to the *back* four or five inches of the hinges, and glue the two hinges to the lid at the back only. Nail the middle and front of the hinges in place—do not nail them too tight, let the hinge nails flex slightly. *Do not glue the hinges along their full length, as this will cause warping of the lid.*

With the lid in the correct position, locate and drill the ⅜-inch-diameter holes for the hinge pins, parts number 5. Do not glue the pins in place until after the box is finished and painted.

Turn the legs and attach them to the chest.

Finish to suit, following the general finishing instructions given in the introduction.

48 ♦ Plant Stand

This book has two plant stands: this one and the more traditional half-round plant stand—Project 49. This one, by itself, is not particularly pretty, but it is functional. This plant stand can be used in places where the half-round stand would not fit. When this stand is in place and has plants on it, it really doesn't look bad at all—if nothing else, it is different!

Instructions

Study the plans carefully. Note how each part is to be shaped. As you study the plans, try to *visualize* how you will make each part and how the project will be assembled. Note which parts you will put together first, second, and so on—exactly how *you* will put it together.

The skirt, part number 4, is irregular in shape and will have to be laid out on a 1-inch grid to make a full-size pattern. Lay out the grid on heavy paper or cardboard, and transfer the shape of the piece to the grid, point by point.

Transfer the full-size pattern to the wood, and carefully cut out the piece. Check all dimensions for accuracy. Sand all over with fine grit sandpaper, keeping all edges sharp. If you are making only one plant stand, simply lay out the pattern directly on the wood.

Carefully cut the remaining parts to size according to the materials list. Take care to cut all parts to exact size except the shelves, parts number 6 and 7—fit these last to the assembly.

Note: The ends of many of the pieces are cut at 6½ degrees. Try to make all cuts with the same saw setting, so that all angles will be exactly the same.

Lightly sand all surfaces and edges with medium sandpaper to remove all tool marks. Take care to keep *all* edges square and sharp.

NO.	NAME	SIZE	REQ'D.					
				5	BRACE	3/4 X 1 1/2 - 10 3/8	1
1	SIDE	3/4 X 4 3/4 - 29 1/2	2	6	TOP SHELF	3/4 X 5 1/4 - 12 3/8	1
2	BASE	3/4 X 1 1/2 - 16 5/8	2	7	CENTER SHELF	3/4 X 5 1/4 - 14 3/4	1
3	BOTTOM SHELF	3/4 X 5 1/4 - 16 1/4	1	8	TOP	3/4 X 5 1/4 - 14 LG.	1
4	SKIRT	3/4 X 2 1/4 - 10 3/8	1	9	FINISH NAIL	6 d	36

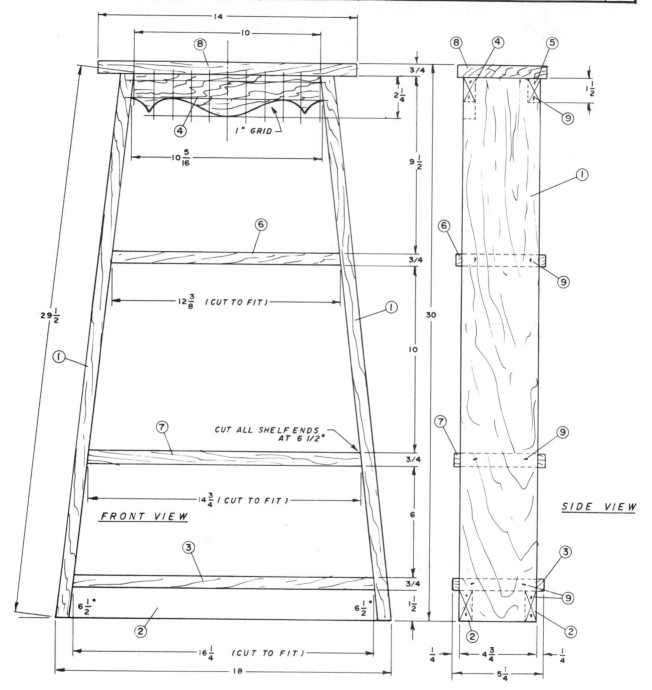

FRONT VIEW

SIDE VIEW

After all of the pieces have been carefully made, dry-fit all pieces except the center shelves, parts number 6 and 7—that is, put the complete project together without glue or nails to check for accuracy and good-fitting joints. If anything needs refitting, now is the time to correct it.

Once all of the parts fit together correctly, assemble the project, keeping everything square as you go. Check that all fits are tight.

After the project is put together, fit the missing shelves, parts number 6 and 7—remember the ends are cut at 6½ degrees.

This project should be painted.

49♦Half-Round Plant Stand

If you visit many antique shops, at least in New England, you will see a few half-round plant stands similar to this one, but most have signs on them, "NOT FOR SALE." The dealers use them to display things and do not want to sell them, because they are hard to come by. When I realized this, I started making them to sell. They sell very fast here in southern New Hampshire. I can't understand why more people don't make them, because they are easy to make and do *not* require much material. The only drawback is that they *are* hard to paint. They are *great*—my wife, Joyce, just loves hers—in fact I had to make her a second one, since she found so many uses for the first.

Instructions

Study the plans carefully. Note how each part is to be shaped. As you study the plans, try to *visualize* how you will make each part and how the project will be assembled. Note which parts you will put together first, second, and so on—exactly how *you* will put it together. On this project it is best if you have a helper, because holding the three legs and trying to glue and nail the thing is a little awkward alone.

You will have to glue up a board ¾ inch thick, 18 inches wide, and 36 inches long to make the three shelves, parts number 1, 2, and 3.

Carefully lay out and cut the legs according to the given dimensions. I tacked the three boards together and cut them all at once. This way they are the same exact size and shape. *Important:* Be sure to keep the 90-degree angle as noted on the plans. *Stop and recheck all dimensions before going on.*

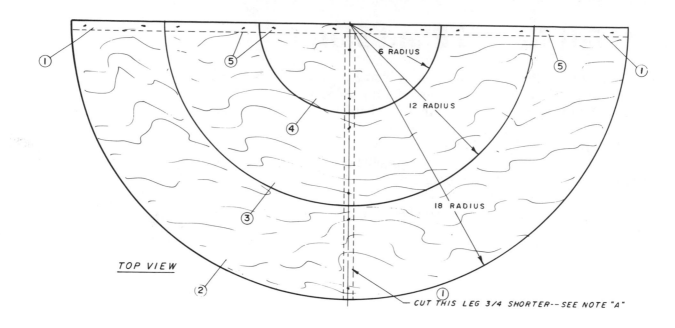

TOP VIEW

6 RADIUS

12 RADIUS

18 RADIUS

CUT THIS LEG 3/4 SHORTER--SEE NOTE "A"

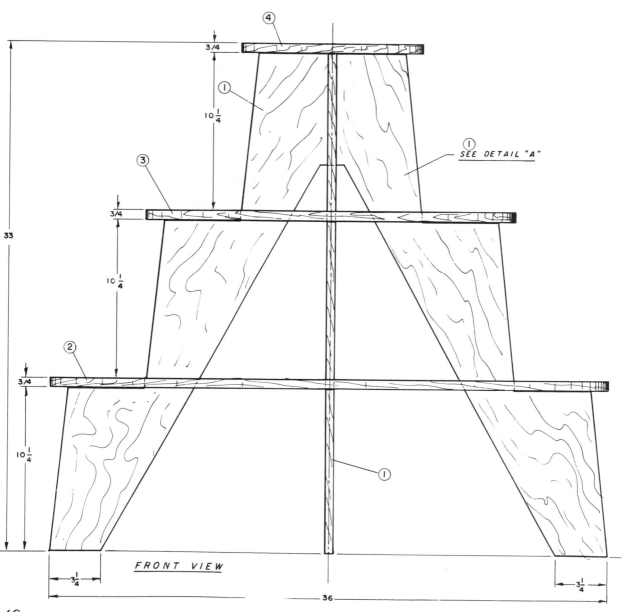

FRONT VIEW

SEE DETAIL "A"

33

10 1/4

10 1/4

10 1/4

3/4

3/4

3/4

3 1/4

3 1/4

36

146

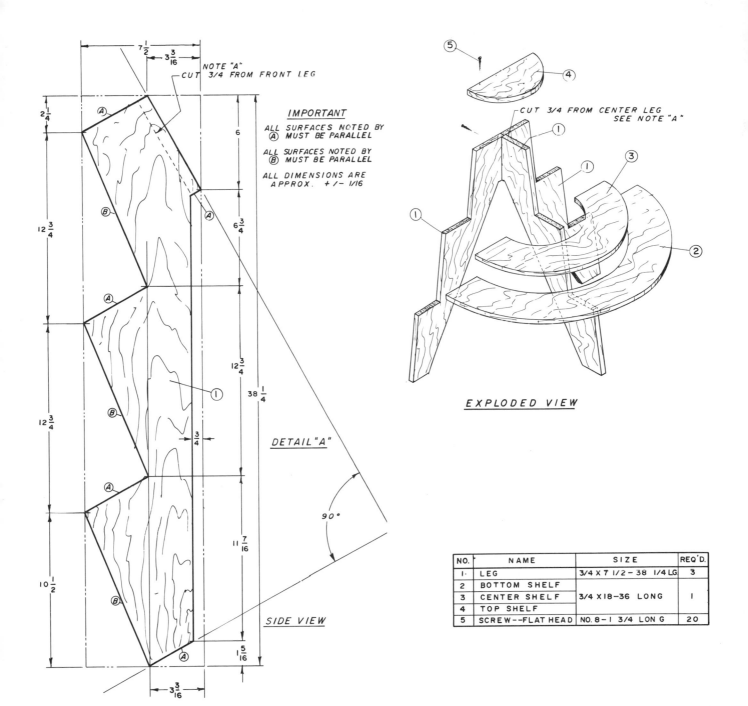

IMPORTANT

ALL SURFACES NOTED BY
Ⓐ MUST BE PARALLEL

ALL SURFACES NOTED BY
Ⓑ MUST BE PARALLEL

ALL DIMENSIONS ARE
APPROX. +/- 1/16

NOTE "A"
CUT 3/4 FROM FRONT LEG

CUT 3/4 FROM CENTER LEG
SEE NOTE "A"

DETAIL "A"

90°

SIDE VIEW

EXPLODED VIEW

NO.	NAME	SIZE	REQ'D.
1.	LEG	3/4 X 7 1/2 – 38 1/4 LG.	3
2	BOTTOM SHELF		
3	CENTER SHELF	3/4 X 18 – 36 LONG	1
4	TOP SHELF		
5	SCREW--FLAT HEAD	NO. 8 - 1 3/4 LONG	20

Lightly sand all surfaces and edges with medium sandpaper to remove all tool marks. Take care to keep *all* edges square and sharp.

Once all of the parts fit together correctly, assemble the project, keeping everything square as you go. Check that all fits are tight.

Finishing

Finish to suit, following the general finishing instructions in the introduction. I have painted some of my plant stands all over; but, I found it much faster if I stain the shelves and just paint the legs—*see* the photograph. Either way, this plant stand will look good.

50 ✦ Victorian Side Table

This side table loosely falls within the broad "Victorian" style of furniture design. It should be made of oak or ash as was much Victorian furniture—and so that it will look like the original. My wife uses her side table as a plant stand; so, today, you can use this project for many things. Because of its attractive style, this table can be used in almost any place or room.

Instructions

Study the plans carefully. Note how each part is to be shaped. As you study the plans, try to *visualize* how you will make each part and how the project will be assembled. Note which parts you will put together first, second, and so on—exactly how *you* will put it together.

The leg ends, parts number 1, will have to be laid out on a ½-inch grid and transferred to the wood. Cut out the two leg ends while they are either tacked or taped together, so that you will have two pieces of the same exact size and shape. Also sand the edges while the parts are still together.

Carefully cut the remaining parts to size according to the materials list. Take care to cut all parts to exact size and exactly square (90 degrees). *Stop and recheck all dimensions before going on.*

Lightly sand all surfaces and edges with medium sandpaper to remove all tool marks.

Make a ¾-inch-wide by ⅜-inch-deep rabbet in the two frame ends, as shown.

After all of the pieces have been carefully made, dry-fit the parts. If anything needs refitting, now is the time to correct it.

Once all of the parts fit together correctly, assemble the project, keeping everything square as you go. Check that all fits are tight.

Finish to suit, following the general finishing instructions given in the introduction.

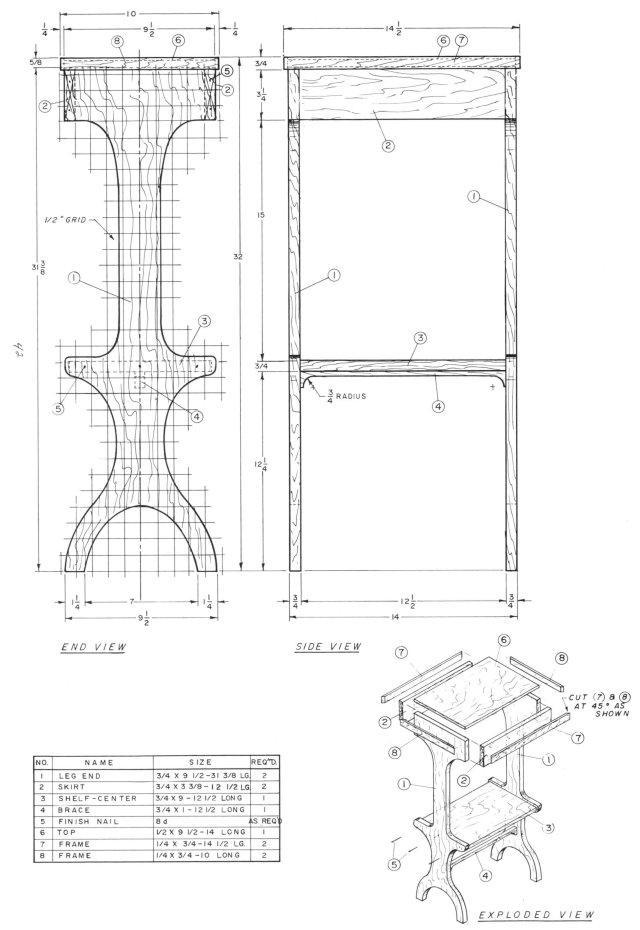

END VIEW

SIDE VIEW

1/2" GRID

3/4 RADIUS

NO.	NAME	SIZE	REQ"D.
1	LEG END	3/4 X 9 1/2 – 31 3/8 LG.	2
2	SKIRT	3/4 X 3 3/8 – 12 1/2 LG.	2
3	SHELF – CENTER	3/4 X 9 – 12 1/2 LONG	1
4	BRACE	3/4 X 1 – 12 1/2 LONG	1
5	FINISH NAIL	8 d	AS REQ'D
6	TOP	1/2 X 9 1/2 – 14 LONG	1
7	FRAME	1/4 X 3/4 – 14 1/2 LG.	2
8	FRAME	1/4 X 3/4 – 10 LONG	2

CUT 7 & 8
AT 45° AS
SHOWN

EXPLODED VIEW

149

51◆Side Table with Drawer

My wife, Joyce, had been after me for some time—months, probably years—to make her a side table for the bed. It had to be made of bird's-eye maple to match the bed. My excuse for a long time was that I did not have any bird's-eye maple wood. My friend, Donald Dunlap, from the line of renowned New Hampshire Dunlap cabinetmakers, gave me some bird's-eye maple in trade for some drawing I had done for him. I loved the wood, but it ruined my excuse against building the side table. This design is a little fancier than most; but the lines are so pleasing that this is the one I had to build—finally.

The canted drawer assembly is somewhat hard to make, but well worth the effort.

Instructions

Study the plans carefully. Note how each part is to be shaped. As you study the plans, try to *visualize* how you will make each part and how the project will be assembled. Note which parts you will put together first, second, and so on—exactly how *you* will put it together.

The top, aprons, and front trim—parts number 1, 2, and 3—are irregular in shape and will have to be laid out on a 1-inch grid or laid out to make full-size patterns. Lay out the grids on heavy paper or cardboard, and transfer the shape of each piece to the appropriate grid, point by point. The top pattern can be simply laid out using a compass and the given dimensions without using the grid.

The top will probably have to be glued up to make the 16-inch-wide piece. Try to match the grain pattern so that the joint will not show. My wife just bought me a biscuit joiner, so I thought I would use it to join the two pieces for the top. It worked *great*—don't know how I ever got along without it. If you don't have a biscuit joiner, you might want to use dowels. Many times I have used simple butt joints for something like this—they seem to work okay for me. Sand the top so that it is very smooth.

Transfer full-size patterns to the wood, and carefully cut out the pieces. Check all dimensions for accuracy. Sand all over with fine grit sandpaper, keeping all edges sharp.

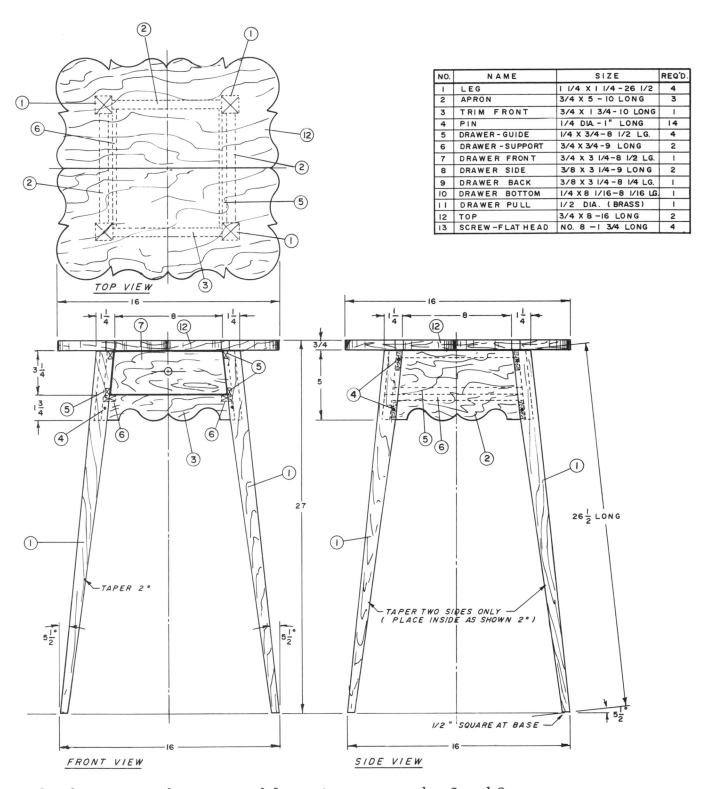

NO.	NAME	SIZE	REQ'D.
1	LEG	1 1/4 X 1 1/4 - 26 1/2	4
2	APRON	3/4 X 5 - 10 LONG	3
3	TRIM FRONT	3/4 X 1 3/4 - 10 LONG	1
4	PIN	1/4 DIA - 1" LONG	14
5	DRAWER - GUIDE	1/4 X 3/4 - 8 1/2 LG.	4
6	DRAWER - SUPPORT	3/4 X 3/4 - 9 LONG	2
7	DRAWER FRONT	3/4 X 3 1/4 - 8 1/2 LG.	1
8	DRAWER SIDE	3/8 X 3 1/4 - 9 LONG	2
9	DRAWER BACK	3/8 X 3 1/4 - 8 1/4 LG.	1
10	DRAWER BOTTOM	1/4 X 8 1/16 - 8 1/16 LG.	1
11	DRAWER PULL	1/2 DIA. (BRASS)	1
12	TOP	3/4 X 8 - 16 LONG	2
13	SCREW - FLAT HEAD	NO. 8 - 1 3/4 LONG	4

TOP VIEW

FRONT VIEW

SIDE VIEW

Cut the tenons in the aprons and front trim—parts number 2 and 3—
according to the dimensions given on the plans and parallel to the ends, as
shown.

Carefully cut the remaining parts to size according to the materials list.
Take care to cut all parts to exact size and exactly square (90 degrees).
Stop and recheck all dimensions before going on.

Lightly sand all surfaces and edges with medium sandpaper to remove
all tool marks. Take care to keep *all* edges square and sharp.

I used a taper jig to cut the taper on the legs. If you do not have one, look

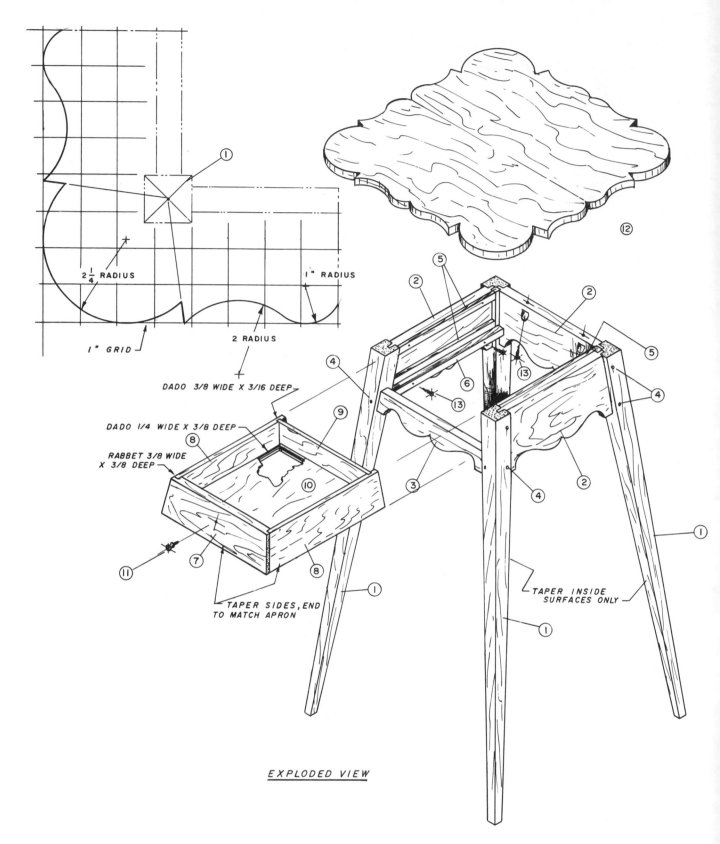

2 ¼ RADIUS

1" RADIUS

1" GRID

2 RADIUS

DADO 3/8 WIDE X 3/16 DEEP

DADO 1/4 WIDE X 3/8 DEEP

RABBET 3/8 WIDE X 3/8 DEEP

TAPER SIDES, END TO MATCH APRON

TAPER INSIDE SURFACES ONLY

EXPLODED VIEW

up how to make a simple jig in a good cabinetmaking book.

Cut the taper for the legs *after* you locate and cut the ¼-inch-wide by 1¾-inch-long mortises for the aprons, parts number 2.

After the legs, aprons, and front trim—parts number 1, 2, and 3—have been carefully made, dry-fit the parts. If anything needs refitting, now is the time to correct it. Glue these pieces together using clamps, as needed.

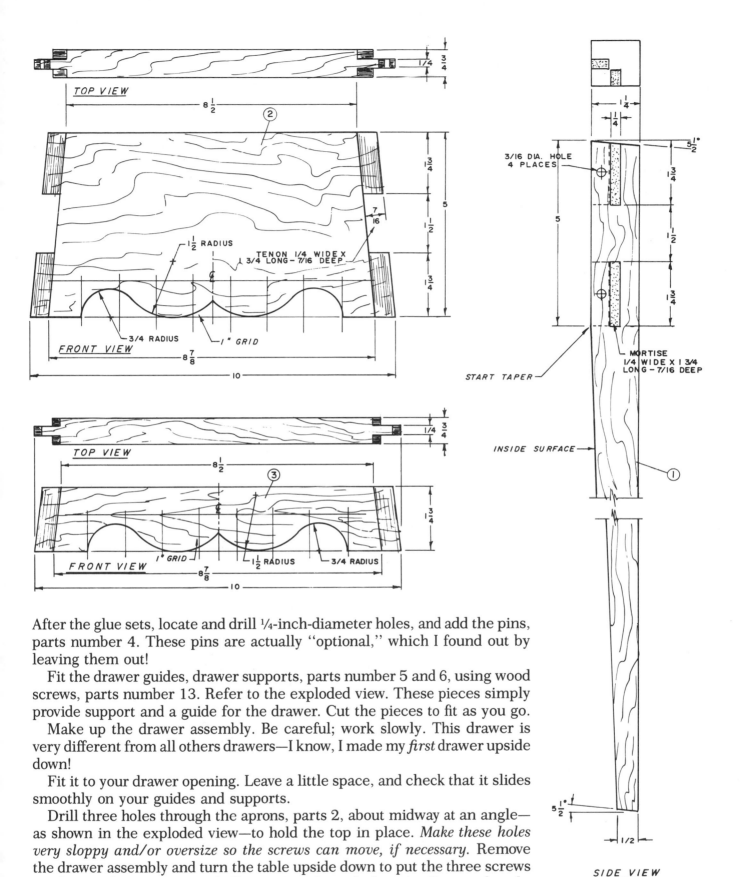

After the glue sets, locate and drill ¼-inch-diameter holes, and add the pins, parts number 4. These pins are actually "optional," which I found out by leaving them out!

Fit the drawer guides, drawer supports, parts number 5 and 6, using wood screws, parts number 13. Refer to the exploded view. These pieces simply provide support and a guide for the drawer. Cut the pieces to fit as you go.

Make up the drawer assembly. Be careful; work slowly. This drawer is very different from all others drawers—I know, I made my *first* drawer upside down!

Fit it to your drawer opening. Leave a little space, and check that it slides smoothly on your guides and supports.

Drill three holes through the aprons, parts 2, about midway at an angle—as shown in the exploded view—to hold the top in place. *Make these holes very sloppy and/or oversize so the screws can move, if necessary.* Remove the drawer assembly and turn the table upside down to put the three screws in place—take care *not* to drill or screw through the top. *Do not glue the top in place—let it float, as it will expand and contract.*

Finish to suit, following the general finishing instructions given in the introduction.

153

52◆Early Open Hutch

As pewter and pottery plates began to replace wooden plates, the open hutch became very popular. At first rails were used to hold the plates vertically—later, grooves replaced the rails. These hutches usually had two or three open shelves at the top to display the pewter and pottery plates and a closed cupboard underneath with one or two shelves to store kitchen utensils. As years passed, open hutches gave way to the more formal china cabinets of the 1800s—as low-priced pressed-glass plates replaced the pewter and pottery plates.

This unusual open hutch was found in southern New Hampshire. It can be made with standard one-by-twelve pine lumber from any lumber yard. Don't let the large size of this project intimidate you; it is just like making a small wall box, except that you are using larger pieces of wood.

Instructions

Study the plans carefully. Note how each part is to be shaped. As you study the plans, try to *visualize* how you will make each part and how the project is to be assembled. Note which parts you will put together first, second, and so on.

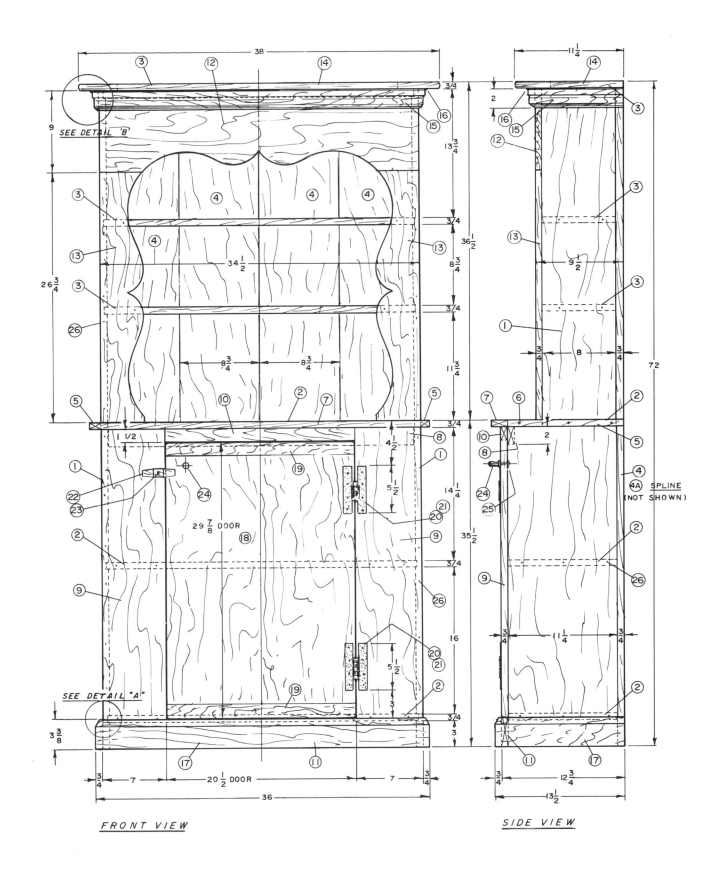

FRONT VIEW

SIDE VIEW

Any parts that are irregular in shape should be laid out on a grid or drawn full-size according to the given dimensions to make full-size patterns. The drawing notes a 1-inch grid for laying out the two front side pieces and the top board—parts number 12 and 13. Lay out the grids and transfer the shape of each piece to the appropriate grid, point by point.

155

NO.	NAME	SIZE	REQ'D.
1	SIDE	3/4 X 11 1/4 - 71 1/4 LG.	2
2	BOTTOM SHELF	3/4 X 11 1/4 - 33 1/2 LG.	3
3	TOP SHELF	3/4 X 8 - 33 1/2 LG.	3
4	BACK	3/4 X 8 3/4 71 1/4 LG.	4
4A	SPLINE	1/4 X 3/4 -71 1/4 LG.	3
5	SHELF EXTENSION	3/4 X 1 1/2 -12 LONG	2
6	PIN	1/4 DIA. - 3 LONG	6
7	SHELF FRONT	3/4 X 1 3/4 - 36	1
8	DOOR STOP	3/4 X 2 - 33 LONG	1
9	FRONT - SIDE (BOTTOM)	3/4 X 7 - 34 3/4 LG.	2
10	TOP DOOR RAIL	3/4 X 1 1/2 - 20 1/2	1
11	DOOR RAIL BOTTOM	3/4 X 3 3/4 - 20 1/2	1
12	RAIL - TOP	3/4 X 9 - 34 1/2 LG.	1
13	FRONT - SIDE (TOP)	3/4 X 5 - 26 3/4 LG.	2
14	TOP BOARD	3/4 X 4 - 64 LONG	1
15	MOLDING	3/4 X 2 - 64 LONG	1
16	MOLDING	1/2 X 1/2 - 64 LG.	1
17	BOTTOM MOLDING	3/4 X 3 3/8 - 64 LG.	1
18	DOOR	3/4 X 20 1/2 - 26 7/8	1
19	BATTEN	3/4 X 1 1/2 - 20 1/2	2
20	HINGE "H" STYLE	3 X 5 1/2 (BLACK)	2
21	SCREW FL. HD.	TO SUIT	16
22	LATCH	5/8 X 3/4 - 3 1/2 LG.	1
23	SCREW FL. HD.	NO. 8 1 3/8 LONG	1
24	DOOR PULL	3/4 DIA. - 3 LONG	1
25	PIN	TO SUIT	1
26	SQUARE CUT NAIL	8d (2" LONG)	AS REQ'D

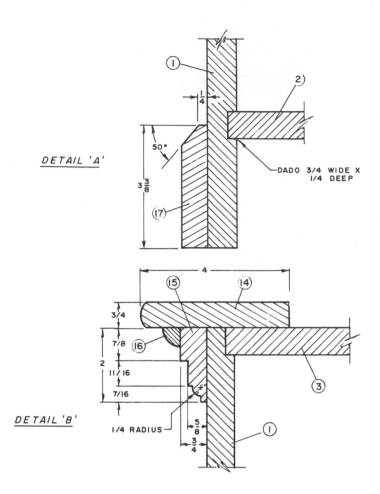

DETAIL 'A'

DETAIL 'B'

Carefully cut all of the parts according to the materials list. Take care to cut all parts to exact size and exactly square (90 degrees). In a project this big, all cuts *must* be at 90 degrees or it will show up. *Stop and recheck all dimensions before going on.*

Lightly sand all surfaces and edges with medium sandpaper to remove any burrs and all tool marks. Take care to keep *all* edges square and sharp at this time.

Lay out and cut the six ¼-inch-deep by ¾-inch-wide dadoes in the two sides—parts number 1. Be sure they are cut at exactly 90 degrees. *After* the dadoes are cut, make the 3¼-inch by 35¾-inch notch for the step in the hutch. Be sure to start the notch, or step, just below the third dado up from the bottom, as shown—this is important. *Be sure to make one right-hand and one left-hand pair of sides.*

Make all the remaining parts and mouldings following the detailed illustrations and given dimensions. Check all dimensions for accuracy, and check again that both sides are exactly the same size. Resand all over with fine grit sandpaper, still keeping all edges sharp.

Cut the notches in the backboards—parts number 4—and add the splines—parts number 4A—as shown in detail "C".

Add the shelves and backboard—parts number 2, 3, and 4—to the sides—parts number 1.

Cut and fit the shelf extension, pins, door stop, front sides, door rail, and top rail—parts number 5, 6, 7, 8, 9, 10, and 11.

Cut and fit the top front sides and top rail—parts number 13 and 12.

Add the top board and mouldings—parts number 14, 15, 16, and 17.

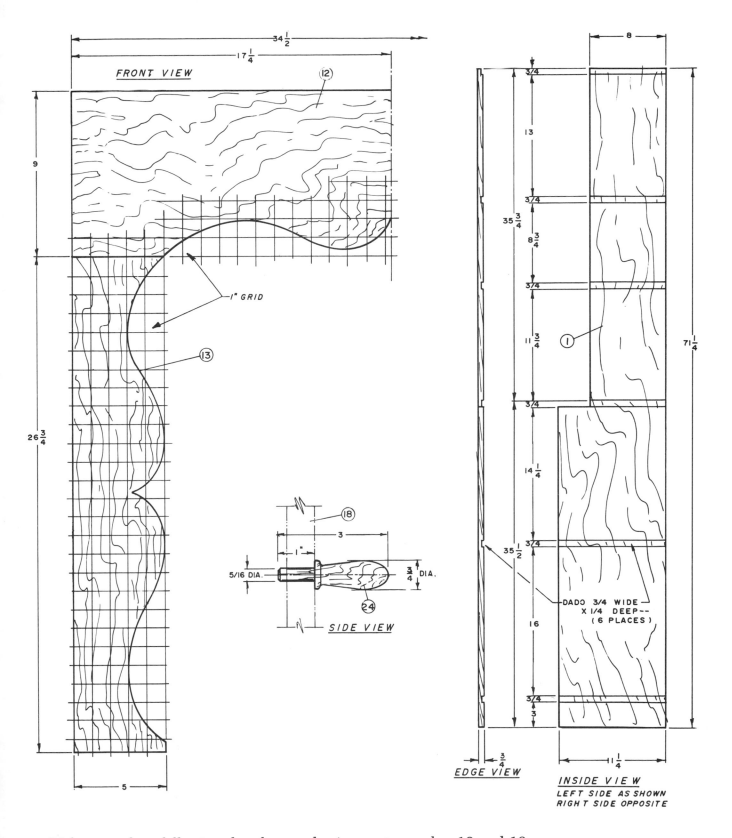

Make up a door following the plans and using parts number 18 and 19. Attach the door to the assembly with "H" hinges, parts number 20—use either 4-inch or 5½-inch hinges. (The original hutch used 5½-inch hinges, but I could not find this size; so I used two 4-inch "H" hinges.)

Turn or shape the door pull, part number 24, on a lathe—or, better still, hand-carve it approximately as shown. The original was hand-carved and very crude.

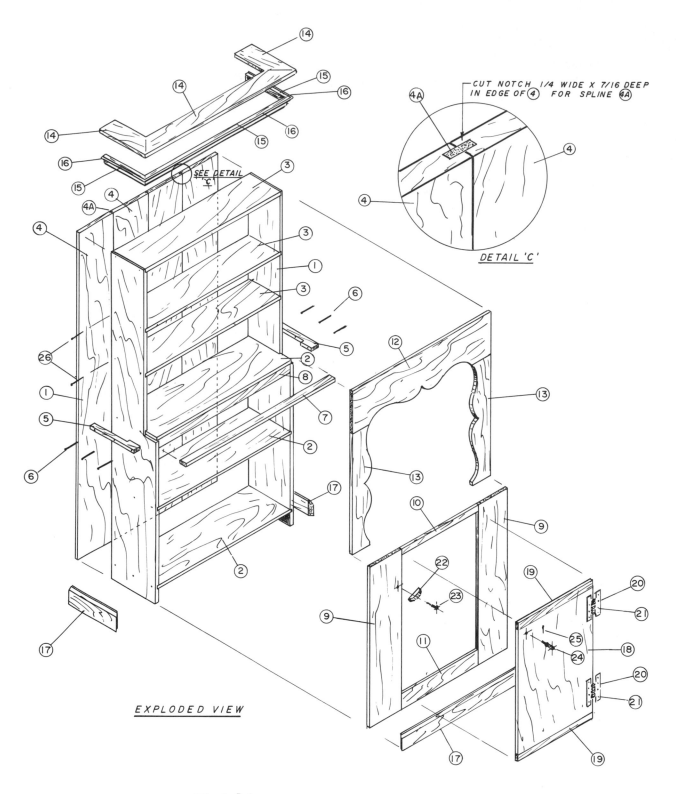

CUT NOTCH 1/4 WIDE X 7/16 DEEP IN EDGE OF ④ FOR SPLINE ④A

DETAIL 'C'

EXPLODED VIEW

Finishing

Finish to suit, following the general finishing instructions given in the introduction.

158

Index

Metric Conversion

Inches to Millimetres and Centimetres

MM—millimetres   CM—centimetres

Inches	MM	CM	Inches	CM	Inches	CM
⅛	3	0.3	9	22.9	30	76.2
¼	6	0.6	10	25.4	31	78.7
⅜	10	1.0	11	27.9	32	81.3
½	13	1.3	12	30.5	33	83.8
⅝	16	1.6	13	33.0	34	86.4
¾	19	1.9	14	35.6	35	88.9
⅞	22	2.2	15	38.1	36	91.4
1	25	2.5	16	40.6	37	94.0
1¼	32	3.2	17	43.2	38	96.5
1½	38	3.8	18	45.7	39	99.1
1¾	44	4.4	19	48.3	40	101.6
2	51	5.1	20	50.8	41	104.1
2½	64	6.4	21	53.3	42	106.7
3	76	7.6	22	55.9	43	109.2
3½	89	8.9	23	58.4	44	111.8
4	102	10.2	24	61.0	45	114.3
4½	114	11.4	25	63.5	46	116.8
5	127	12.7	26	66.0	47	119.4
6	152	15.2	27	68.6	48	121.9
7	178	17.8	28	71.1	49	124.5
8	203	20.3	29	73.7	50	127.0